My

BEST
DAY-USC
TROJANS FOOTBALL

*A collection of responses from former & current
football athletes from the
University of Southern California*

949-645-8109

MARK KEYS

Always
Mark Keys

M
C K
C E
O Y
O S
L

PRESS

McCool Keys Press
5308 Neptune Avenue
Newport Beach, CA 92663

Individual Sales. This book is available through most bookstores or can be ordered directly from McCool Keys Press at the address above.

Quantity Sales. Special discounts are available on quantity purchases by corporations, associations, and others. For details, contact the " Special Sales Department " at the publisher's address above.

Printed in the United States of America.

Library of Congress Cataloging-in-Publication Data is available from the publisher.

ISBN 978-0-9893000-0-1

The author and publisher assume neither liability nor responsibility to any person or entity with respect to any direct or indirect loss or damage caused, or alleged to be caused, by the information contained herein, or for errors, omissions, inaccuracies, or any other inconsistency within these pages, or for unintentional slights against people or organizations.

DEDICATION

I would like to dedicate this book to Fred Howser, USC Class of 1958, for always being there, supporting me personally, as well as with this USC book version of My Best Day.

ACKNOWLEDGEMENT

I would like to thank the following people for their support:

My wife, Laurie, my daughters Page and Megan, my mom and Don, my dad (who attended USC) and Ellen, My mother-in-law Glenell & Frank, Dan, Nancy & Tyler Stringer, Rick John, Dan & Michelle Parke, and as always, the inspiration provided by the memory of David "Bucko" Shaw.

John Hamilton, thank you for the support, contact information and being there for me during all of my pop ins.

Tony Horvath, Ron Lamberton, Joe Bockrath, Paul Salata, Michelle Nguyen, Dr Safman, Dr Carlson, Dr Yaru, Dr Greywall, and all my other doctors, and Start Physical Therapy.

Also thanks for the support of JK McKay, Pat Haden, Tim Tessalone, Matt Curren, Shane Foley, Paul and Allison McDonald, Fred Pierce, Sam Dickerson and all the players and coaches who supported and contributed to this book.

FOREWORD

When you are a Trojan, every day is a "Best Day".

When USC is part of your genetic makeup, there are no bad days. Trojans are different from everyone else. We hail from a University that is truly special and different, and we take from this great institution our own part of the Cardinal and Gold fabric. So, wherever we go in life and whoever we meet, we know we have had the great fortune of walking the paths of Troy. Not many people can claim that.

USC football players, coaches, and staff are the finest in the nation. They always have been and they always will be. They have played in the biggest games and produced some of the game's greatest traditions and moments. Those Trojans who have suited up and stood on the Coliseum side line are the best of the best. This book provides a glimpse of how Trojans think. It takes a snapshot of the top memory of those who have worn the Cardinal and Gold.

I think you'll find these vignettes enlivening, inspiring, and refreshing. I know I did. It's great to be a Trojan. Fight On!

— **MICHAEL GARRETT-USC**

Tailback 1965
Heisman Trophy winner 1965
USC Athletic Director 1993 - 2010

INTRODUCTION

In May of 1991, I injured my back while working and was placed on permanent disability. Prior to my first back surgery, I had my picture taken with Magic Johnson of the Los Angeles Lakers. Later, Blaine Skinner, a friend of mine who works for the Lakers, was able to get Magic to autograph the snapshot. It made my day.

As a hobby, I began writing other celebrities asking for autographed photos. Their positive result amazed me. During the next several years, while incapacitated with several more back surgeries, knee surgeries, and ankle reconstructions, I collected even more autographs.

One day while walking, I noticed the magnificent beauty of a simple blue sky. Upon returning home, I thought about what a good day it was despite my back problems. I felt great, and it struck me: I wondered what all those people I had been receiving autographs from felt was their "best day". I received hundreds of responses,that have evolved into several "my best day" books.

Expanding on the "best day" book theme, my focus on athletes from USC was a natural evolution for me since I am a huge USC Trojan fan.

I have loved USC football and the school, ever since my dad, who attended USC, took me to my first USC vs

Notre Dame Football game when I was five. I still have the program from that game. I have gone to games on and off over the years ever since that first game. My dad took me to games in the 60's and the wonderful games of the 70's to watch JK McKay, Anthony Davis, Pat Haden and the rest of the wild bunch. I attended six USC Rose Bowl Games in person and I never tire of the thrill I get seeing the Trojans come out of the Coliseum tunnel. My wife, Laurie, comes from a family of Trojans as well. Her parents attended USC, and her mom was voted Miss March USC in 1958. Laurie's paternal grandparents graduated from USC as well. Her grandmother, Marjorie Edick Parker, was Helen of Troy her senior year. USC has a rich tradition in their athletic programs and a fiercely loyal alumni group. FIGHT ON!

My Best Day was my last home game. We were playing our crosstown rivals, UCLA, at the Coliseum. The emotion and feelings were overwhelming in the locker room before the start of the game. I was a senior in my final home game in the Coliseum. I remember wanting to have such a great last game, but I fumbled so much. I remember fumbling the ball four times. I did score a touchdown and rushed for 219 yards. We ended up winning the game, 22-21. After we won, I loved running off the field and being saluted by the USC crowd. It was great. The feeling when the seniors were saluted during the last home game, it was incredible.

— MARCUS ALLEN

Tailback 1981
Heisman Trophy Winner
College and Pro Football Hall of Fame

My Best Day was probably my sophomore year at USC when I played against Oregon State. Statistically you'll find it wasn't my greatest game, but it was the one in which I proved to myself I could play major college football. That was exciting for me.

— **MIKE GARRETT**

Tailback
Heisman Trophy Winner 1965
USC Athletic Director 1993-2010

Personally- any holiday or wedding when the great majority of our family is together enjoying each other.

Professionally- the day we at USC beat Ohio State in the 1985 Rose Bowl.

— **TED TOLLNER**

Head Football Coach 1983-1986

Watching our freshman class (John McKay's 1st year) evolve game by game and as juniors, winning the National Championship and the Rose Bowl.

Needless to say, the Wisconsin game was the ultimate. While I got the trophy for Player of the Game, we had 40-50 guys that it could have gone to; and to the coaching staff. They had us very well prepared.

— PETE BEATHARD
Quarterback 1963

My Best Day was the Rose Bowl, 1975. It was my last game and I was a Senior. I thought it was my last game as a player, due to being accepted to Oxford as a Rhodes Scholar. While at USC, I was blessed to play in 3 Rose Bowl Games. In the final Rose Bowl Game, we were playing Ohio State for the National Championship. Back then, the game was a big deal: the Pac-8 vs. the Big 8. I threw a winning touchdown to best pal, J.K. McKay, Jr. and then went for a two-point conversion, to Shelton Diggs for the win. The result was USC being National Champions. Final score: 18-17

— **PAT HADEN**

Quarterback 1975
USC Athletic Director

USC vs. UCLA football in 2001 doesn't rank up there with my wedding day or the birth of my children, but as for my most recent "Best Days" it sure qualifies.

— **PETE CARROLL**
Head Football Coach 2001-2009

Greatest day, huh? Game day running through the tunnel is always a great day. More specifically it would have to be ASU vs. USC 1990. It was homecoming for me. I grew up in Arizona, and the game was at ASU. There had been interviews by opposing coaches & players making negative comments about me leading up to the game, regarding why I didn't stay in Arizona. I was the 5A Player of the Year a few years earlier, and some people didn't like me leaving the state. In pregame (warm up), an opposing player told me that they had put in plays specifically for me. I did not like that.

So, with about 60 friends and family there to watch me and the hundreds more on TV, I picked off their star quarterback (who was NFL bound) two times. I had double digit tackles. My favorite part was blowing up their 245 pound tailback (1st round NFL Draft choice) on 4th and 1 for a 2-yard loss. They came at me all day...on purpose... and I kicked their ass and we rolled them. I was MVP.

PS- the post-game interview was comical, when someone asked their head coach about my effort!

Greatest Day! FIGHT ON!

— **MIKE SALMON**
Defensive Back 1993

My Best Day (regarding USC Football) was fortunately catching a touchdown pass against Notre Dame in the 1955 game in the Coliseum

— **DON MCFARLAND**

Receiver 1955

My Best Day was September 25th, 1954 before or after a game. I cannot remember who we played. But there was one wild day that I will always remember. Bing Bordier and his future wife, George Galli and his future wife, Marvin Goux and his future wife, myself, and my future wife, Norma, all went to Santa Barbara for a wedding. Norma and I got married in the Santa Barbara Courthouse, by a judge who was a friend of Marvin's (he was a Santa Barbara boy). My knees were knocking; the ride was hurried and frantic. We barely got there in time as the judge was busy. My wife, Norma, and I now have 3 grown kids, and lots of beautiful grandkids. We just had our 50th anniversary...and it brings back that hectic but wonderful day 50 years ago.

— IRWIN SPECTOR

Right Guard 1954

Every day is my Best Day

— **FRANK GIFFORD**

Halfback, 1952
Pro Football Hall of Fame
Television Announcer

My best day occurred when I met Nick Pappas! You see, Nick recruited me from a high school in Hawaii. He was not the pressurized, fast-talking, ever-promising recruiter. He saw that I was a boy of Samoan, Hawaiian-Chinese heritage, that had never been away from the Islands, and lived in very humble means. He understood what the value of family was in my life, and enveloped me with his family... his wife Deedee, and three young daughters were now my family. He opened his home to me, he helped me to adjust to college expectations, and life in the big city. He did not spoil me with material things, but instead had me babysit his three girls when he and Deedee had USC functions. I welcomed this, as I had three younger brothers at home in Hawaii, whom I missed very much.

I could always take my problems to Nick and he would take the time to help me find a solution. He encouraged me and provided me with thoughtful advice, yet he had the most wonderful sense of humor. What more can a young man want from a Father Figure? To me, he was Mr. USC, always portraying the love and spirit of our school.

My wife (a Part-Hawaiian girl and USC Alum) feels so indebted to the Pappas Family, for their many kindnesses and favors to me. Even as newlyweds living off-campus, they were there to help us with our first baby boy...how to change diapers, feed, bathe our new baby, etc. They have always been interested in our well-being, and it continues to this day. When my wife and I celebrated our 50th wedding anniversary, he and DeeDee came to our gathering in Hawaii. As you can see, it was my Best Day when Nick Pappas came into my life the first days at USC, and how he continued to be my mentor and hero through 60 years of his wise and trusted counsel.

— **CHARLIE ANE**

Offensive Lineman 1952

My Best Days-take your pick- No particular Order:

- Getting Married
- Kids
- Touchdown in Rose Bowl as an 18 year-old freshman
- Getting out of the air force
- Graduating from College- USC 1949
- Mom at debutante ball
- Making it in a Pro Bowl for the SF 49ers
- Spending a day with President Ford
- 1st Super Bowl

— **PAUL SALATA**

Wide Receiver 1949
founder "Irrelevant Week"

As an athlete: scoring the first and then winning run in an eight-run final inning victory to overcome a seven-run deficit in our league championship game...way back in 1973 as a senior in high school.

As a parent: watching any sporting event in which my three children are involved.

As the sports information director at USC: the privilege since 1979 of being able to come to work every day at Heritage Hall and provide a service to all the athletes, coaches and staff who make the USC athletic department the special place that it is.

— **TIM TESSALONE**

USC Sports Information Director

My Best Day happened 58 years ago, September of 1950, the day I transferred from Notre Dame to USC. I remember it like yesterday, waiting at the gate of "Bovard Field" for the Trojans to finish practice so I could ask for a chance to walk on.

The answer was yes from Coach Jeff Cravath and I became a part of the "Trojan Family". I was a starting defensive halfback for two years under Coach Jess Hill and played with Frank Gifford, Lou Welsh, Charlie Ane, Jim Sears, Lindon Crow, Rudy Bukich, Al Carmichael, Marv Goux, and Sam Tsagalakis to mention a few. I also had an interception and key knockdown in the USC victory over Wisconsin in the 1953 Rose Bowl Game.

— **HARRY WELCH**
Defensive Halfback 1953

My Trojan Best Day occurred on November 30, 1968 when we played #9 ranked Notre Dame as the Coliseum. We were undefeated and ranked #2 behind Ohio State, who was also undefeated. Notre Dames' All American Quarterback, Terry Hanratty, was injured, so starting for them that day was a sophomore QB by the name of Joe Theismann. We kicked off to ND to start the game and they began their first offensive series on their own 20 yard line. On second down and seven yards to go, their All American wide receiver, Jim Seymour, ran a short out pattern. When Theismann, who was being pressured by the "Wild Bunch's" Charlie Weaver and Al Cowlings, threw the pass, I broke in front of Seymour, intercepted the pass and returned it for a touchdown, putting us up 7 to 0. What ND didn't know was that Coach McKay had grilled into me that in 2nd and 3rd down short yardage situations ND's favorite play was the short out to Seymour. I actually ran the route better than Jim on that play! That coupled with the fact that Joe couldn't see me because of the rush by Charlie and Al led to my "Best Day" as a Trojan. Unfortunately, we tied the game 21-21 and later lost to Ohio State in the Rose Bowl. (PS-Joe Theismann recounted the same play in his Autobiography years later)

— **SANDY DURKO**

Defensive Back 1968

I went out for football at USC in 1948. My goal was to make the training table as there were about 150 guys going out for the team. I made the training table but I wound up on the scout squad.

Coach Cravath would call up for Kirby. I'd come rushing up, coach would say I want the other Kirby (Jack. Jack beat me out. I had to leave the team because I reinjured my kidney.)

— **KIRBY GALT**
Defensive Back 1951

I guess I have had a lot of good days at USC. But, I believe my best off the field was when Coach Jesse Hill told me I had been elected Co-Captain of the 1954 USC Team.

I think I would have to say that on the field was my senior year when I played the full sixty minutes and scored three touchdowns against California. I think that might have been the last time anyone at USC played a full sixty minutes, never coming out of the game.

— **LINDON CROW**
Defensive Back 1955

I have had many great and fun filled days and have a lot to be thankful for. My first thought was the day I decided to attend the University of Southern California. At the time I did not understand the impact it would have on the rest of my life. This decision allowed me to earn a business degree, play football and meet life lasting friends, and work and live in Southern California which is the best piece of real estate in the world. I have a wonderful wife (Debbie) and three beautiful children: Kayleigh, Shannon, and Trey. I guess my "Best Day" is very subjective, I really feel there have been so many it wouldn't be right to single out just one.

Fight On!

— SCOTT TINSLEY
Quarterback 1982

My best FOOTBALL day (births of children and marriage don't count) was in September 1981. We (USC) played Oklahoma which pitted number 1 versus 2 in an early season clash. Oklahoma came out fast, lead through three quarters, and looked like they were going to win easily. In the fourth quarter, we had worn them down and made a comeback, that resulted in us being on their four yard line and down by four.

The next play was a pass play that I had an option to run a 15 yard cross or block and delay over the middle. I checked with the quarterback (John Mazer) and we agreed to delay. As the play developed, I came off the block, but the pass was high and I could only get a hand on it knocking it down. I didn't realize Marcus Allen was open behind me and I tipped the winning touchdown away from him.
The next play, Coach Robinson sent in the second string tight end to replace me, telling him to run the 15 yard cross. He got to the huddle and took out the other wide receiver by mistake, leaving me still in the game. We called the same play and everyone went to Marcus and the other tight end, which caused Mazer to scramble. I flowed with him and was wide open for an easy throw and catch to win the game with 4 seconds left. I was a hero for a day on a play that I wasn't even supposed to be in on.
GOD IS A TROJAN. Fight On!

— **FRED CORNWELL**

Receiver 1981

I have been fortunate enough to have had many great moments. Two stand out:

The first being the 1955 USC vs. Notre Dame game. We here heavy underdogs and I was fortunate to score 28 points (a record) and we beat them handily.

A tie with that day would be the 300 plus yardage game I had against the Chicago Bears when I was with the L.A. Rams. We broke an eleven game losing streak against them.

These were both second to the day I realized there really was a God.

— JON ARNETT

Running Back 1955
College Football Hall of Fame

My Best Day was January 1st, 2004 at the ceremony during the Rose Bowl Game. USC won our Rose Bowl game against Wisconsin in 1953. I set a record for completions and was awarded the MVP Trophy, becoming the only Pacific Coast Player to win the award in the last 13 years against Big 10 teams. I received a trophy, and a plaque. The wall plaque, behind the Giant Statue at the entry to the Rose Bowl reads. "Rudy 'The Rifle' Buckich".

— RUDY BUCKICH

Quarterback 1953

My Best Day would have to be January 1st, 1953, in The Rose Bowl game against Wisconsin. (we won 7-0). I was the back-up punter. Prior to the game we were going through our warm-ups as usual. Then as we return to the field, the stands are now filled with 90,000 plus fans, the announcer starts introducing the Trojans.

My "Best Day" was walking out on the Rose Bowl field to the cheering fans. It's just awesome...

— **LARRY CHAFFERS**

Punter 1953

My Best Day—too numerous to count- Best days are when you and others, whether they be family (grandkids-especially now); loved ones; friends, or in my case, football players, realize we are "on the same page". What we are experiencing is special, and that "life has few moments such as this." It happens often if you believe in other folks you're doing it with, and they believe in you. Then you will often say" "Life has many moments such as this"

My USC best day is encapsulated into a Best Season:

1) January 1962: Coach McKay called me into his office, and said he was looking for a coach to "run" his defense. (Coach does not employ "coordinators"). Did I know of any coaches I've run across in my short career. I mentioned two, but coach said they were entrenched. I told him I would go home and try to come up with more names. In the morning, at the encouragement of several friends close to me, I went and told Coach McKay and told him I had the man, "me". Coach McKay said. "You've got it."

2) February 1962: Linebacker Damon Bame decided to become a Trojan (I had recruited him and had coached him at Glendale College) instead of a Bruin. He was a 2-year All-American.

3) May 16, 1962: My son, Mike W. Giddings was born, and Coach McKay dedicated that day's spring practice to him.

4) All 1962: USC goes 10-0 , allows only 55 points, plays Wisconsin in Rose Bowl for National Championship. USC wins. Bame was the "heart" of the defense.

5) Spring 1963- Dr Norman Topping, USC President: a) he called in the top gynecologist from Britain for an operation for Mike W's mom, and it was successful. b) Dr. Topping takes the staff to a luxury dinner, thanking us for helping raise money time and again for his University Park project (which today is USC modern campus)

All in all, quite a day. During the 1962-1963 school year, USC won a record five National Championships in sports.

— **MIKE GIDDINGS**

Assistant Football Coach 1961-1965

My Best Day was actually the day that Coach John McKay personally called me while I was at work at Leon's Men's Store on 17th Street in Costa Mesa. That was Christmas week 1963. I was actually working during Christmas vacation at the store when the phone rang. To my disbelief, Coach McKay asked me, "Mike, how would you like a full football scholarship to USC? I will ask that you play one more season at OCC and then we want you to come up in the Spring. Until then, please call Bonnie West next week and come up to fill out the forms. So, what do you think, Mike?" Oh my goodness! As an eager 19 year old athlete, it was the best and most exciting news I could have asked for at that time in my life. This then young mad dropped the phone and jumped for joy...I'm sure it was over a 40" vertical jump.

I was offered over 50 football scholarships out of Anaheim High School in 1962, **but not one from USC.** So, I took an appointment to the United States Naval Academy. Because I did not have trigonometry or physics in high school, I had to attend Orange Coast Junior College for one year prior to entrance to the Academy. As it happens, I played for first-year head coach Dick Tucker and we had a great year. My teammates were so good that I was even named a JC All-American at running back. We lost only one game that year and it was to Santa Ana JC, who eventually won the Junior Rose Bowl game. Fortunately, OCC won the Junior Rose Bowl the following year against Northeast Oklahoma. This past year I became the second Football Hall of Fame player to be inducted at OCC. What an honor...but that phone call...wow!

I was very blessed to have played at USC in that era. At 5'9" and 150 pounds, it was an exciting adventure and the personal phone call from Coach John McKay will always be my USC Football-Best Day!

— MIKE HUNTER

Defensive Back 1962

My Best Day is any day spent with my wife, children, and grandchildren, in this the greatest nation on earth. Probably my best day in sports was January 2, 1963, the Rose Bowl game, in front of 101 thousand in Pasadena. It was my first network assignment as play-by-play for NBC radio. Final Score: USC 42 vs Wisconsin 37…a game rated as perhaps the best in Rose Bowl history.

Little did I realize that three years later I would be living and working in Los Angeles as "The Voice of the Trojans". I've been a sports announcer for 55 years and I'm in the Southern California Sports Broadcasters Hall of Fame, so I've been blessed with many "best days".

— MIKE WALDEN

USC Sports Announcer

Although I had good games against Ohio State and Notre Dame, my Best Day was the USC vs. Tennessee game in the 1940 Rose Bowl.

USC beat Tennessee 14-0. I was the 3rd string quarterback for USC that year; after a knee injury the year before; and then hurting it again in the beginning of the current season. I was able to redeem myself by calling my own plays to score a touchdown on a 70-yard drive. I then threw a 90 yard touchdown pass to Al "Antelope" Kruger for our final score.

— AMBROSE SHINDLER

Quarterback 1940

In the fall of 1955 I played red squad (JV's) for USC. Jon Arnett (All-American) and C.R.Roberts were the stars of USC Varsity.

For personal reasons I dropped out in 1956. I returned in spring of 1957. I made the team in 1957. Even though it was a poor season we had many great coaches and players. Coaches: Don Clark (head coach) Don Doll (all-pro) "the" Al Davis (end Coach) Marv Goux (a legend) George Dickerson our offensive coordinator who played behind Johnny Lujack at Notre Dame. I attended Don Doll's funeral this year and George was there. In his 90's and still smoking cigars.

Notable players were Mike "Tarzan" Henry, Willie Wood, Don Buford, Ron Mix and Rex Johnstone to name a few. Mike & Marlin McKeever were on the frosh team.
My claim to fame was winning the Sam Berry Award in 1955 and scoring the 1st TD of the season against Michigan in 1957. We struggled with new coaches, a new system, and the loss of starters because of Pacific Coast Rules. Stanford and UCLA went after USC.

I served in the Air Force and married Penny in 1959-we are still married with 4 kids and 5 grandkids.

When I applied for a job in the stock market in 1959 my boss looked at my resume, and the fact that I attended USC was all he cared about. He & I became partners for 15 years. USC football was the beginning of many best days.

— **BILL HOWARD**
Halfback 1957

I was disappointed that I was not originally voted into the first USC Hall of Fame. Once I was inaugurated into the USC Sports Hall of Fame I was extremely grateful and exhilarated.

— **HAL BEDSOLE**

Tight End 1963

Best Day: 1970 USC vs. Notre Dame
USC was a 14-point underdog to #1 Notre Dame. USC wins, Joe Thiesman sacked in the end zone, he fumbles, I recovered to score a touchdown! (this was the only year I played defense) (1971 All-American)

Best Day: Everyday my kids hit a homer, strike out a batter, make a block, made a tackle, scored a touchdown, slammed a point, digged a ball, scored a point & rebounded a ball.

— JOHN VELLA

Offensive Tackle 1971

Life brings with it many good days as well as many very difficult ones. I've had my share of both, but your request for me to remember my "Best Day" has brought to mind many of the great ones. I grew up in Southern California where my life was dominated by the sun, friends, and an ability to play football. The day I was given an athletic scholarship and asked to become part of the USC Trojan family was a great day for me. By the time I graduated, USC had given me an education, life long friends, a national championship ring, and good memories as part of football's greatest tradition. I had many incredible days at USC, but none I would call that, "best one".

My Best Day came 46 years ago at a small Baptist church in Costa Mesa, California. I accepted Jesus Christ into my heart that day and gave Him the control of my life. That day was the best day of my life.

Welcome to the best day of your life!

— **BRAD GREEN**
Offensive Lineman 1979

I have had two "Best Days", running through the Coliseum tunnel for the first time in 1952 and kicking an extra point in the 1953 Rose Bowl Game against Wisconsin 7-0.

The number one "Best Day" was kicking a 38 yard field goal in the last 14 seconds to defeat an undefeated Stanford team 23-20 and being carried off the field by my teammates in November, 1953.

— **SAM TSAGALAKIS**

Kicker 1954

When I married my wife and playing USC Football opened a lot of doors for me.

    — **DON DOLL**

      as told by Diana Doll
      Halfback 1948

Every day when I wake up.

— ANTHONY DAVIS

Tailback 1974
College Football Hall of Fame

Clearly, sixty intervening years make it easy to identify my "Best Day" as a Trojan, and to separate it from all the others. That "Best Day" was October 25th, 1948 (USC vs. Cal) It stands out, not because of personal statistics or the national significance of the game (such as ending Notre Dame's 21 game winning streak on December 4th, 1948) but because of the events preceding the game, the importance of the SC-Cal rivalry (not UCLA in those days) to SC Alum and supporters, the pre-game hype, and the frenzy of the Cal student body (the most obscene of that time) that players like to silence.

Cal's record at game time was 4 and 0, while ours was 3-0-1, with an October 4, 1947 tie with Rice.

Two weeks before the game, we defeated Ohio State 32-0. On the train after the game, in the middle of that celebration, Braven Dyer, an L.A. Times sportswriter who covered SC football dropped by, noticed our frivolity and shouted out that we shouldn't get too high on ourselves because in two weeks we would have to travel to Strawberry Canyon to play Cal. The party then got interesting. During the exchange, Dyer blurted out that he would bet each of the players a new shirt that they couldn't beat Cal. The players responded with an uproarious acceptance of Dyer's proposal.

After a 48 to 6 victory over Oregon State and two weeks of hype, the game was finally played under a beautiful blue sky before the first ever sell-out crowd of 81,000 plus in Strawberry Canyon, including thousands of loud, frenzied, profane and ill-mannered Cal students (believe me, free speech started at Cal before the 1960's)

Cal received the opening kickoff and scored almost immediately on a 65- yard running play. We responded with a nine-play drive to tie the score. During that drive, there was one stretch where we ran the same play five consecutive times. It was a play over Cal's right tackle where I was responsible for kicking out the Cal end. I not only made the block all five times, I pancaked the end twice, and the play made good yardage each time. Probably the most satisfying series of plays in my life. We scored again to take a 13-7 lead, but Cal came back in the second quarter to go ahead 14-13. Then, midway through the second quarter, we went on another drive for a touchdown that I scored, and which put us ahead for good, 20-14. On the ensuing kickoff I went down on the coverage and hit the kick returner so hard that he never returned to the field. The most important thing about the hit was that it really fired up the SC players who were close enough to hear it. Minutes later we went in for halftime intermission fired up and anxious to get back on the field and finish Cal off. After the intermission, our kick returner, Don Doll, took the second half kickoff and returned it 95 yards for a touchdown and a 27-13 lead. Game Over. Cal was whipped. Our reserves scored twice more for the final 39-14 score.

Within a week or two of the game, each of the 37 players who got into the game received a new shirt from Dyer. Years later, he admitted that the 37 shirts cost him $185.00, and that it took him some time to make it up on his expense account.

Dyer later authored a book entitled "Ten Top Trojan Thrillers" in which he described this game as "Thriller No. 10". "Thriller No. 2" in that book was the December 4, 1948 SC-Notre Dame 14-14 tie game which ended Notre Dame's 21 game win streak. I guess that the ND game doesn't seem as 'big" to me as the Cal game, because we won the Cal game and should have won the Notre Dame game but didn't. The Cal game in 1947 was very satisfying in many ways, while the ND game in 1948 was disappointing. ND scored the tying touchdown with 34 seconds to go, but only after a "questionable" pass interference penalty gave them the ball on our two yard line.

Final Note: In the Cal game of 1947 we hit a peak in performance that we never reached again. In the end, sportswriters selected ND #1, Michigan #2, and USC #8. However, in the 1948 USC-ND game, our 14-14 tie knocked

ND out of the #1 sport and a third consecutive National Championship.

— **BILL BETZ**

Fullback 1948

My very Best Day was fifty years ago when I married my wife, Joan. We have four charming daughters Lucy, Lori, Carol and Ellen.

Also another best day was when I enrolled at USC in 1946, after being discharged from the US Marine Corps, and played football during the 1946 and 1947 seasons, and I finally graduated in 1948.

— **WALLY SEMENIUK**

Offensive Guard 1948

It is always so nice when anyone remembers those days gone by when I was a Trojan. It seems that as great as our past Trojan Teams were these young kids of today have taken it to another level of greatness. It makes us old guys proud.

In regards to my Best Day, that would have to be November 19, 1997 the day my son Jason was born. Sharing that moment with my wife (who did all the work), mother and sister was a feeling so emotional and positive I find it hard to describe. It brought so many thoughts and feelings of family and hope.

I thought of being a father and of the relationship that I had with my own father. I remember how I began playing football to gain the attention of a father I wanted to have as a part of my life. How as my career in football progressed it became the glue that held together a family that was falling apart. All those hopes and dreams that went into becoming USC's all-time leading receiver were really about love and family.

— **RANDY SIMMRIN**
Wide Receiver 1977

My Best Day was the USC / UCLA game in 1945. I intercepted one of Ernie Case's passes in the midfield and returned it to the Bruin 42. Seven plays later, Ted Tannehill scored USC's opening touchdown. Later, when the Bruins had scored their first tally and were red-hot in the third quarter, I crashed through and heaved Skip Rowland for an eight-yard loss back to the Bruin 24. On the very next play, I grabbed Case's pass and carried back six yards to the Bruin 23. Two plays later, Tannehill scored the touchdown which clinched the game at 26 to 7.

— JOE BRADFORD

Defensive Back 1946

I had some wonderful challenging experiences at USC and beyond. Even though I started for three years as fullback for the Trojans and blocked for two Heisman Trophy winners, played in two Rose Bowls was a first round draft pick in 1968, my "Best Day" (Football wise) was in Spring 1965 when I was trying to make the team. We must have had five high-school All-Americans, and an additional five others like me who were merely All-Leaguers, fighting for one position in the backfield to block for Mike Garrett (who ended up winning the Heisman that fall). I was sixth team, behind some great fullbacks/halfbacks all who could get the job done. We were in the final scrimmage, I did not expect to play at fullback or halfback as the others with bigger names were getting more time. Then it happened as I was feeling alone and neglected on the sidelines, Garrett went down with an ankle sprain. And I heard John Mackay holler out "where's Hull?" I simply could not believe he was calling out my name, he had not talked to me all spring and I was not even on the depth chart as they only noted the top five. I thought he had forgotten all about me. I even thought he may have been coughing, you know, "HUFFFFF, cough, cough, "something like that.

Well, he said it again, "Where is Hull????" I still could not believe it, one of the assistants ran over to me with a Cardinal Jersey, the kind only starters wore and told me to put it on and get the heck out there. I remember stepping into the huddle, all these "men", seniors and all league and hot shots snorting, bleeding and sweating; and I fresh and clean as a daisy and just off the sidelines. The tight end asked me my name; the QB also did not know who I was. McKay said, "Give him the ball, let's see what Hull can do with it". The rest is history. I drove up the middle for a notorious 3 yards, on the next play I leveled the linebacker so the fullback could break outside. And then the next play they gave me that ball again and I broke outside for about a 30 yard gain, the longest of the whole scrimmage.

— **MIKE HULL**

Fullback 1968

It is an honor to be asked to write about my best day. It is special to be part of the Trojan Family and to be part of the heritage, tradition and history of USC football. I realize how fortunate I am to have received two degrees from the University of Southern California and it is a privilege to serve on three boards at my alma mater today. I have many great memories from my time at USC and I am blessed to experience the Trojan Family every day in work and the lifelong friendships I have built with other Trojans. I also learned to always Fight On regardless of the circumstances.

There are several best days I have had in my life including marrying my best friend and the birth of our two sons. However, my best day as a Trojan would have to be getting my first start as the USC quarterback my senior year in 1990. I had significant opportunities to play prior to getting my first start, including throwing the first touchdown pass against Ohio State the year before in the Coliseum. Going into my senior year, our team had won three consecutive PAC-10 Titles and played in three consecutive Rose Bowls. My senior year we were facing some adversity and we had lost a pivotal game to Washington in Seattle early in the season. We had most recently lost to Arizona at the Coliseum and we were facing a must win situation in a road game against Arizona State. On Monday of game week, Coach Smith stopped practice and called the team up to let them know that I would be starting against ASU.

It was awesome to have the team rally around me and my first opportunity to start.

It was a special day for me. My father traveled over to the game and Mike Giddings, my high school coach from Newport Harbor was there as well. I had been preparing my entire career for this moment. The game was a low-scoring, hard fought game. The coaches called a conservative game plan and we executed it by controlling the ball and time of possession. We had two running backs get knocked out of the game with concussions so I was asked to do more; passing and running when called upon. It was a great feeling to be out there just playing football, competing, and leading my teammates!

I love the game of football and there was nothing better for me than playing quarterback. I always took a lot of pride in the preparation of the game, studying tendencies and looking for little things that could help us win. We controlled the game that day even if the final score did not indicate a dominant win, it was a tough battle won at a time when we really needed it. In the end, we won 13-6 and I was named the Chevrolet ABC Player of the Game. It was rewarding to know that the time I spent preparing for that moment had paid off and I was able to lead the Trojans to victory! Fight On!

— **SHANE FOLEY**

Quarterback 1990

My Best Day in football in the 1944 season was scrimmage on Bovard Field. As a result my teammates shared my feelings and we went on to an undefeated season. We became Rose Bowl Champions playing against Tennessee on January 1, 1945. I was fortunate to catch a pass from Jim Hardy for a touchdown. The final score was 25-0.

Most of our team was in the Military: USNROTC, Navy V-12 and Marine V-12. I believe there were three civilians on our team. About half dozen went on to Pro-Careers.

Our grandson, Blake Spenser is in the business school at USC, we are such a proud Trojan Family. FIGHT ON!

— **DOUG MACLACHLAN**
Receiver 1945

It was a typical day of southern California football this early December afternoon at the Coliseum - calm winds, sunny, and about 72 degrees. That's what I call perfect "football weather" having grown up a San Gabriel Valley native! What was different about this day though was it would be the last home game for my son, Michael McDonald, a USC backup quarterback and holder for field goals and extra points. Senior Day is a great tradition for the Trojans as it honors those football players who have committed themselves to countless hours of practice, meetings, off-season workouts and games for up to five years to compete at the highest level of college football. So, on this day players, their proud parents as well as the fans tend to reflect on the previous four or five years.

I was very fortunate to have experienced some of the same Senior Day feelings as Michael having played from 1976-1979 for the Trojans earning a National Championship as part of the '78 team (25 years before Michael would earn a ring as part of the 2003 team). These feelings are indescribable as memories of plays, players, coaches and opponents flash through your mind leading up to the game and during warm-ups on the field. Also, we both had great success during our playing days which heighten those emotions. During my two years as a starting quarterback, we only lost one game, won the title as mentioned in '78 and finished second in the nation in '79, my senior year. Michael one-upped me by winning 2 National Titles in '03 and '04 and had a higher passing efficiency rating than me even though he did not start. In fact, his first 2 passes were for touchdowns, which Sports Information Director, Tim Tessalone believes is a NCAA record!

What is even more gratifying for me was that I got to broadcast those two touchdown passes by Michael from the USC radio booth as the color commentator for USC football alongside my play-by-play partner, Pete Arbogast. I almost fell out of the booth on the first one against Arkansas at home when the Trojans were up by a score of 63-17. When the play action pass came down from the booth, from the young and aggressive Offensive Coordinator, Lane Kiffin, we were all simultaneously stunned and delighted! My kid's first time on the field as a QB after being awarded a scholarship during fall camp resulted in a TD pass, his first ever! What a thrill! To this day, I say Lane Kiffin is my favorite coach as he is the one who called the pass to allow my son to complete it for a score. We interviewed Michael on live radio after the feat and our sideline commentator, John Jackson suggested to Michael that he did it just like his dad used to. Michael's response was "my dad never looked this good", a great comeback for my self-assured, fun-loving son.

During the start of Michael's time at USC as a walk-on quarterback in 2003 I was on the field gathering information prior to our broadcast of the game and I noticed Head Coach, Pete Carroll playing catch with his son and Tight End Coach, Brennan Carroll as he did before every game. My initial thought was "how cool is that"; my next thought was "why can't I do this with my son"? And so, I suggested playing catch during pre-game warm-ups to Michael, and he thankfully, agreed. We threw it around during every home game, and when Michael started traveling during the '04 season we played catch everywhere – from South Bend to Pro Player Stadium during the National Championship game against Oklahoma to the many Rose Bowls played by the Trojans. It was a "Field of Dreams" experience for those fathers who wish they had a chance to play catch one more time with their son. The only difference for us is we were able to perform this very personal experience together in front of tens of thousands of people every weekend during the season!

And so, back to December, 1st 2007 for Michael's last home game in the Coliseum as a senior, which happened to be played against UCLA just like my last home game in 1979. It was also, the last time we were able to toss the ball at the Coliseum with one another after four plus years of doing so. As I made my last throw for a touchdown to

Michael, I thought back to those touchdowns I threw to Kevin Williams, Calvin Sweeney, Danny Garcia, Vic Rakhshani, etc. during my playing days. Finally, I walked over to give my son one last hug and wish him luck before he entered the locker room in final preparation for the game, and also to tell him how much it had meant to me that he allowed me to play catch with him. His response which brought tears to my eyes was "it meant a lot to me too, Dad". It was truly my Best Day!

— PAUL MCDONALD

Quarterback &
USC Football Announcer 1980

It was the first home game of the 2005 season against the SEC foe Arkansas. It was the start of my 3rd season with the Trojans, but my first game coming off being awarded a scholarship in the off season.

I was slotted as the 3rd string QB behind Matt Leinart and John David Booty; and yet to see any game action in my 2 previous season. The closest I had come to getting on the Coliseum turf was tossing the football around with my father, Paul McDonald former USC All American QB and current radio color analyst, hours before kickoff. This was a special tradition we started my Freshman year, and have played catch on every field SC played on from 2003-2008. From The Rose Bowl to South Bend to South Beach for the FedEx Orange Bowl... If you were in the stadiums an hour and a half before the game, you would've seen Paul and Michael McDonald running around playing catch as if it were the front yard of my parents' house.

So many of you Trojan fans remember the beating we shelled out to Arkansas in 2005. It was one of those games where every play call that came in worked to perfection, and our defense didn't give them a chance to breathe. We could do no wrong on offense, and Arkansas could do no right. We led 42-10 at half with no signs of slowing down.

After a few quick scores by the good guys to start the half, it was time to start thinking about pulling the starters.

This was JD Booty's time to shine. He quickly led the team down for a couple scores, racking the score up to 63-10.

This is when I started to sweat. But with Arkansas in possession of the ball and a fresh set of downs with around 2 minutes in the 4th, chances are they would run out the clock. But with an interception by a young (future Rose Bowl Defensive player of the game) linebacker Kaluka Maiva put the SC offense back on the field. And as I looked towards JD Booty I hear "Magic, you're in!"

I rushed over to Coach Sarkisian to get the play call and trotted onto the field. With no time to think, I focused on remembering the play call and not tripping over myself on my way to the huddle. After 2 successful run plays I get the next play call from Sark..."move to near rt A26 Y-Box." Play action pass play!?! Kiffin called a pass play with 43 seconds to go with a 63-14 lead! I must have floated the 20 yards back to the huddle to deliver the play to my fellow 3rd stringers.

I call the play and we line up on the 4 yard line with 43 seconds to go. Ball is snapped and I fake the handoff and find Jimmy Miller in the back of the end zone for a touchdown! I joins my teammates in the end zone to celebrate and try to take in the fact that my first pass in the Coliseum was for a touchdown.

The icing on the cake was listening to the playback of my father calling my touchdown play. Hearing the joy and pride in his voice made me feel so thankful to be able to share that experience with the person I look up to the most.

That was my best day as a Trojan.

— MICHAEL MCDONALD
USC Quarterback 2005

My Best Day as a player at USC was when at Notre Dame, as an offensive lineman, I was awarded the Offensive Player of the Game and awarded the Gabrielson Trophy for that achievement. Although we lost that game and Randy Tanner had his leg broken with a compound fracture on the opening kickoff, I managed to stay in my game, with great concentration and mechanics, to pound offenders any chance I had. The Notre Dame fans were very cordial should I say after the game; they congratulated me and other players who played well, instead of boasting their victory, which was very exciting on a beautiful fall day in South Bend!!

— JEFFREY BREGEL

Guard 1986
Consensus All American

My last year of football at Southern California was in 1952. We had a very good season. We ended up winning the Rose Bowl, New Year's Day, 1953. Twenty-five days later I graduated From USC. All three of the events combined made graduation day "My Best Day"

— **DAVID JIM PSALTIS**

Defensive Back 1953

I really can't say what my best day was...I was Truly blessed to have so many. Go USC!

— **EARL McCULLOUGH**
Wide Receiver 1967

The year 1998 was my senior year. USC vs Notre Dame and it was a homecoming game. This was a very defensive game. Notre Dame Linebacker Kory Minor intercepted a Carson Palmer pass to put the Irish at the USC 14 yard line. The very next play the Irish player was able to get the ball to the 2 yard line and was going for a touchdown and as he was tackled the ball popped loose. I was there to scoop up the ball and return it to the USC 29 yard line. Notre Dame never got closer than the USC goal line the rest of the night. The final score was USC 10- Notre Dame 0. USC had not posted a shutout of Notre Dame in the series since 1962 . That night needless to say I was extremely happy!

The next day the San Gabriel Valley Newspaper read: "Ken Haslip may have come up with arguable the games' biggest play near USC end zone on one of the Irish few scoring chances."

I am honored to be a graduate of USC and to have played football for the Trojans. FIGHT ON!

— **KEN HASLIP**

Corner Back 1998

I have had so many great memories and experiences it is hard to single out just one.

The day I met my future wife in front of my Fraternity on 28th Street was pretty cool.

My first game in a Trojan uniform was memorable. It was 1968 and we opened up against Northwestern, back in Chicago. I was on the kick off team and was the first guy down the field and made the tackle. That is about the only thing I can contribute to the highlight reel as I played behind Jimmy Gunn for most of my career. That was well before title IX and we had 110 guys on full scholarship. Mike Holgren is a prime example of a high school All American QB who chose the wrong school. He could have played anywhere else but USC or "Tailback U" as it was called. He could throw the ball better than Jim Plunket, who he beat out for the high school shrine all American team. Jim goes to Stanford and they build the offense around him, Mike comes to USC where we have the greatest tailback in the nation in OJ. I could go on and on about the talent pool at USC the four years I was in school, but that would fill 10 pages.

Running down on the kickoff team against Ohio State in the 1969 Rose Bowl in front of 100,000 screaming fans was as exhilarating as it gets.

Watching OJ Simpson break off that incredible run to win the UCLA game in 1967, off the block of my two fraternity brothers, Ron Yary and Mike Scarpace was fantastic, even if I was on the bench all of that year.

Getting run over by a freshman fullback named Sam Cunningham in the spring game my senior year was not so cool, but certainly memorable.

I know that I am most thankful for the total experience. I lean back on how tough double days were when I am having a rough time. I say to myself...I made it through that, I can make it through this. Those years molded me into the man I am today and it taught me to always do my best when called on to do so. Never let your fellow man down if you can help it. It taught me that no matter how great you think a person is, he is only human and vulnerable and needs a friend that will cover his back; go into the trenches with him. Marv Goux taught us all that and I never forgot it. That is why Bobby Chandler visited OJ and we all prayed for Bubba Scott when he had cancer. And we were all there to lay Bobby to rest when it was his time to go. It is that Cardinal and Gold blood that courses through your veins because of what we all went through together. I would give the shirt off my back for anyone of my teammates because I know he would do the same for me.

— GREG GEORGE
Linebacker 1970

It was the Rose Bowl games of January 1, 1940 when USC beat Tennessee 14-0. Joe was captain of the USC team that ended the season undefeated and un-scored on. According to news reports, Quarterback Amby was the real star of the game. But quoting Bob Ray, Los Angeles Times Sportswriter:

"But the Trojan player who was the recipient of the most praise from his mates and coaches alike, was Captain Joe Shell, SC's blocking back. Shell played the greatest game he's ever played for Southern California, said Jeff Cravath and Bob McNeish, assistant coaches. 'His blocking was marvelous. He boomed 'em'"

Joe was given the game ball, signed by all the players. He treasured that ball so much he preserved it in a glass case.

That was the last game for Joe, and Amby too, but the two remained close friends, visiting a couple times a year until Joe passed.

— JOE SHELL

as told by his wife Mary
Blocking Back 1939

It was the year the American Football Coaches Convention was in San Francisco. I answered the phone around 11:30 am while working around the house. It was Craig Fertig and he asked if I was planning to attend the Coaches Convention; and I told him I hadn't planned on attending. He then said I might want to change my mind since John McKay was looking forward to talking to me about a full time coaching position at the University.

I arrived around noon the next day and met Craig at 3pm to meet Coach McKay in his suite. We met for approximately 1 ½ hours and when we came to the close of the meeting, Coach McKay offered me a full time coaching position on his staff at the University of Southern California.

And you ask me what was my "best day, USC Football?" I accepted!! Go Figure!!

— **DICK BEAM**
Football Coach 1972-1975

My Best Day in respect to USC Football was in August of 1992 when I tried out for the USC Football team as a freshman. I made the team as a walk-on Quarterback; becoming the first Trustee Scholar (full academic scholarship) at USC to play varsity football. I played under Coach Smith and Coach Robinson, and my friends continue to ask me about my time with the Mighty Trojans to this day.

— RUSSELL BJORKMAN

Quarterback 1995

My Best Day may be somewhat of an odd and insignificant one in terms of USC Football history but I'll never forget my first tackle. I was a Redshirt Freshman and I finally made my way on the special teams. It was one of our first games of the season, against UNLV. We didn't play very well and the game was pretty tight well into the 4th quarter. From what I can recall we were beginning to feel a bit tense as it seemed we may be on the verge of an upset. Fortunately we had just scored to pull ahead and needed a big stop to put the game away. I don't remember much of what I was thinking at the time, or even really how I did it, but I sprinted down on kickoff, through the wedge and SMASH! I crushed the returner at the 15. I actually didn't even realize I made a tackle because it all happened so fast but I remember crystal clear the roar from the crowd and the mob of teammates that attacked me with enthusiasm. Not sure how many were in attendance that day but in that moment it felt like 100,000. For those whom never experienced this it is hard to explain other than it probably one of the best feelings ever. I was so beside myself from the rush. It was almost as if all the energy in the crowd burst though me in an instant. As simple and meaningless as that play may have been, it's a moment I'll never forget.

— **FRANK CARTER**

Tackle 2000

I have had a few best days:

- Won the Rose Bowl Football game 1939 Duke 3, USC 7
- National Championship 1939
- Elected to Dave Collier's Mid Century top 11
  All American Football players in the last 50 years
- Married 67 years

— HARRY SMITH

Offensive Lineman 1939
College's First Half Century All American
College Hall of Fame

Publishers Note:
The Collier's team of eleven members included the legendary Jim Thorpe, Red Grange and Bronko Nagurski among others. The coach was Knute Rockne.

My Best Day didn't have much to do with USC Football. My space flight to Skylab, and particularly the launch, was my "Best Day".

However, I will confine my thoughts to USC Football, and describe my best day within that context.

I was playing freshman football at USC in the fall of 1950 for Coach Ernie Smith. I was a "walk-on" with more enthusiasm than good sense at 155 pounds. Some of my team mates were Jim Contratto, Parry O'Brien and Desmond Koch. My position was second or third string left halfback on offense and defense.

One day, Varsity Coach Jeff Cravath, totally exasperated with his junior varsity, called Coach Smith and told him to bring his freshman over to Bovard Field to scrimmage the varsity. The junior varsity just wasn't cutting the mustard. So, full of trepidation, we frosh went to Bovard and set up our defense against All American Frank Gifford and his cohorts. On about the second play I saw that, on the snap, a hole started to open on the left side of our defensive line, and the line backers moved to it and were immediately smeared. I was just behind the line backers and knew that whoever came through the hole was mine. Sure enough, it was Gifford, and we collided. The match up was like a fully loaded dump truck and a volkswagon bug. I got tangled up in his legs and brought him down and then got up wearing my helmet sideways.

It was then that I had my epiphany. I realized that if I planned to live to fly airplanes I probably should not try to play football at USC after my freshman year. It was a good decision. Gifford had better not try to tangle with me in the air.

— GERALD P "JERRY" CARR

Defensive Lineman, 1950
NASA Astronaut, Commander of Skylab4

I am a first generation Armenian American and I always remember my immigrant parents surprising me by showing up at our first practice at SC. They were looking through the chain link fence around Bovard Field. No way would they have imagined their son going to a major private University on a scholarship. I really made them proud.

My other best day was USC vs. Cal our 3rd game of the season. Cal had gone to the Rose Bowl 3 previous years in a row. The score was Cal 13- USC 7 with 47 seconds left in the game. Frank Gifford was the QB for that game (he wasn't a good QB) but a very good running back. It was generally considered that I was to be a red shirted my first year and since the game was almost over I didn't have my helmet with me. Jimmy Sears yells at me "they want you". I grab the 1st helmet I could find and you are right, it's a defensive lineman's way too big helmet. But I am in the game exactly on the 50 yard line on 3rd down. I connect on a 17 yard pass play to the left, call the exact pattern to the right with 35 seconds left. I hit again to the right with 19 seconds left. My 3rd pass was into the end zone. There was a pass interference call, giving us a 1st down on the 1 yard line. If we score and kick the score would be SC 14-Cal 13. I'm a hero and Gifford has gray hairs.

Well, it wasn't meant to be. Ralph Price (fullback) and I miscommunicate and Les Richter the Cal Linebacker drops me back at the 9 yardline. There was one play left; quick pitch out to Billy Bowers to the four, game over.

I will always wonder had we scored would I have Gifford playing defensive back, he was not a Quarterback.

— ED DEMIRJIAN

Quarterback 1952

Choosing my best USC day is not an easy task. I experienced great days in and around USC as a coach's kid; as a player, a fan, and now as an administrator. I saw the 1962 National Championship; Fertig to Sherman in 1964; played on the greatest team ever in 1972; and caught two touchdown passes during the 1974 SC 55 – 24 win against Notre Dame. But, my best day came in my last game and on my last play as a Trojan. On January 1st, 1975 I caught a 38 yard touchdown pass from my best friend, Pat Haden, with 2:03 remaining in the game and after the 2-point conversion we won the game 18-17 over Ohio State. As a result we won the National Championship and my best friend and I were named Co-Rose Bowl MVP's. It doesn't get a lot better than that!

— JK MCKAY JR.

Wide Receiver 1975
USC Assistant Athletic Director

My Best Day being a part of the USC Football Team should be answered in plural. There was never a time, during the years, that I didn't appreciate my good fortune. I will get to the best day, but first a brief note should be explained. As a high school kid in Columbia, MO I was contacted by a number of schools in the midwest & south. With my high school coach being a great player at the University of Missouri, it was conceded that I would go right to Missouri. Dan Fourot, the Head Football Coach, already told me of his plans that I would be the center he counted on; being 6'2" and 220lbs (big for a center in 1939). However, at the time, there were very few football teams in the country which were on a National Radio Network and heard all over America. Each year I was able to hear Notre Dame & USC; my father and I listened each year, hearing Bill Stern calling the game. As a result, I dreamed of USC; but little ever thought about going there. USC seemed out of my league. Surprise-one day a letter came from guess who? Southern California, offering a full football scholarship. The rest is a life story. One day prior to practice starting, in 1939, the coaching staff (with Howard Jones) took we freshman to see the Coliseum. Though it scared us to death seeing it empty-I knew I was in the Big Leagues.

— **DICK DANEHE**

Center 1941

My Best Day wasn't really much and was, in fact, in the evening. It was our opening game of the 1954 season against Washington State in the Coliseum. As a sophomore I had won the starting job at fullback/linebacker. This was a big deal for me because, as you know, back in those days freshmen could not play on the varsity and that team had their own team and schedule. We also had to go both ways back then. So starting as a sophomore was big. The Coliseum was packed and of course I had never played before 75,000 people or so. Being a "hick" from a small town and small high school (Colton), the whole atmosphere was almost overwhelming. During our warm-ups I was thinking what a thrill to be here and how lucky I was to be a part of this and to be attending and playing for one of the premier universities in the nation. To top it off, we beat a good Washington State team. I played well and scored a touchdown. My folks had come to their first college game and my younger brother ran down on the field after the game and jumped into my arms. Thus began my football career at USC and a night I shall never forget.

— **WAYNE KURLAK**

Fullback 1957

To say my best day at USC would be definitely two situations. Catching the winning touchdown vs. UCLA, when everything was up for grabs in the LA Coliseum in 1952 (USC 14- UCLA 12). Winning the Pacific Coast Conference Championship and securing a trip to the Rose Bowl.

My 2nd situation, was catching the only touchdown scored in the January 1952 Rose Bowl game vs. Wisconsin (USC 7- Wisconsin 0) and winning the Rose Bowl Championship.

— **AL CARMICHAEL**
Halfback 1952

I must say that my best football day at USC was the day Coach John McKay asked me why did I enjoy everyday so much? My response was that one day I would be able to tell others what a great time it was playing football for USC and the friendships I still maintain today. My greatest or best day was in 1972 after winning the National Championship we (the team had a party at Julie's) and Coach spoke to the class for the last time. He said look around you and enjoy every second because you as a group will never be together in one room again. I still hear his words to this day. On the field, when I returned my first punt in Los Angeles against WSU and thinking I could do this again, and I did it two other times in my career.

— DANNY REECE

Defensive Back/Corner 1975

My memories go beyond USC to my time with the 49ers and with the NFL as an official. Of course there are many thoughts about USC, but one time that always stands out-the time when I first did well enough to make the team.

We were playing Cal in the Coliseum, in 1948. Cal was favored and their big star was Jackie Jensen, All-American. I had only played a few minutes in each of the previous games, and because we were losing 13-0 it didn't look too good for me to get in the game.

While sitting on the bench, I either read the end coaches mind, or heard him thinking out loud (Bob Winslow), "I need an End". I immediately raised my hand and looked him in the eye. He looked at me, then away for someone else, and then "OK Nix, get in there"! There was about 13 minutes left in the game.

My first play on defense called for me to close tight. I tackled the Cal running back named Jack Swaner. It shocked me to hear my name echo around the stadium as having made the tackle. Next play, Jackie Jensen went back to pass and no one blocked me. I got him for an eight yard loss. People cheered. Jensen looked at me as if "we'll teach this guy a lesson". His next play appeared to go off in the opposite direction from me, but something told me to get as deep as their deepest runner, and low and behold, here came their speediest runner, Keckly, on a reverse, and I tackled him for a 12 yard loss. The stadium was really cheering.

Cal punted and our halfback, Jack Kirby made a good return putting us in good field position. In the huddle, our QB Jim Powers looked at me in the huddle and said, "this one is for you, you earned it". It was a deep pass. The linebacker held me at the line of scrimmage, and when I got loose, I thought no way Jim is going to throw it to me, but I ran the pattern anyway. When I looked back over my shoulder, the ball was arcing down towards me and I caught it and was tackled on the 3 yard line. Next play our halfback scored and we were in the game. The On-side kick didn't work; the game ended 13-7 and Cal went on to play in the Rose Bowl. After that game, I played every game and went on to be drafted, the next year, by the 49ers.

— **JACK NIX**
Receiver 1950

I know this may seem "over-the-top" and a bit silly, but every day was a "Best Day" for me at Troy. Was it the day former Long Beach Poly head coach turned USC assistant coach Dave Levy offered me a full ride? Or my first day of spring ball when I was the thirteenth quickest guard on the depth chart? Or was it making the offensive green team alongside the gold and red teams? Was it pulling and leading tailback Ron Heller on "right-I-Gee-26 Power" to a touchdown, knocking down Iowa Wally Hilgenberg on a National Championship Squad? Was it earning a starting berth at quick guard my senior year. Or was it John McKay calling me over from his field tower to ask how I was after a bout in the infirmary? Was it eating at train table and having Marv Goux drop by and talk football? Was is playing racquetball with former Trojan and Ram tight end Marlin McKeever? Was it Coach Ray George in my face after missing a block, spraying me with his redman chaw? Was it winning the Alumni Club Scholarship Athletic Award? The Willis O. Hunter Award for the senior USC athlete with the highest GPA? Was it playing buncombe into the wee hours with Hudson Houck, Damon Bame, and Freddie Hill? Was it AD Mike Garrett years later comping me tickets to a Cal game in the early 90's when I was a principal at Placer High in Auburn, CA, and getting to sit with his family? I am now, and forever will be indebted to USC for all the "Best

Days". I still hold on to all those moments. Again and again and again---every day was a "Best Day".

— TOM JOHNSON

Offensive Line 1962

I had a lot of best days when I was at USC. Obviously on of my "Best Days" was when I met my wife, Marianne-we have been married 40 years.

But on a football note; my personal best day was one Saturday afternoon at the Coliseum in 1967; the year we won the National Championship. OJ Simpson was injured; I think it was the second quarter and I played the rest of the game. I gained over 100 yards on 18 carries and after the game Coach John McKay gave me the game ball. I still have the ball and it brings back some great memories.

— STEVE GRADY

Tailback 1967

I have had many Best Days, but the best day probably began when I received a scholarship to play football and run track for USC in 1952. That was the beginning of several beautiful opportunities for me. It was a thrill to play with and against so many great athletes, and achieve a wonderful education. After graduation, and a hitch in the military, I went into law enforcement. Eventually I ended up as the Chief United States Probation Officer for the Federal District of Nevada. I've had a great family life and am now retired.

— **FRED PIERCE**
Halfback 1955

Although I don't feel that anyone should rest on their laurels, the accolades I received helped me to now be able to assist in raising funds to keep the USC Marching Band performing. As a football player I had the most kick returns, most yards gained, was player of the game against both UCLA and Notre Dame; a big thing for a Trojan. In Baseball I had a great mentor in USC's Rod Dedeaux while on the US Olympic Team. I enjoy helping good causes, others and currently raising funds for the USC Marching Band- the Greatest Marching Band is the history of the Universe.

— **REX JOHNSTON**

Special Teams 1959

My Best Day at USC was the day I signed my scholarship. I grew up a USC fan, my grandfather played in the late 1920's under Howard Jones. I remember as a kid going to all of the USC home games with my father who kept the season seats my grandfather had after he passed away. I always loved football and always dreamed of playing for USC. I also was a Rams fan and grew to love John Robinson because of his connections to USC and the Rams. When he came back to USC and I had the opportunity to play for him it was a dream come true. It was especially good because in high school I was offered a scholarship at USC by Coach Larry Smith but I could not get into USC at that time because I did not have the grades coming out of high school due to teenage ignorance. I sat out a year after High School; and went to community college to get my AA degree. I was a Junior College All-American in 1993. I was offered a scholarship by USC again, this time by Coach Robinson and accepted. This was my best day. I also have some great memories while at USC; including playing at Notre Dame and our Rose Bowl clinching win at Oregon State in 1995.

— **RICHARD BEATIE**

Offensive Tackle 1995

The day I was told I would be receiving a football scholarship to attend the University of Southern California was my best day. No one in my family had gone to college.

— ROLLY PULASKI

1958

The motivational strategy of leather helmets will never again be used in football. And it appears that players suggesting plays to a coach on the sideline will never again be used. Everything comes down from "upstairs" these days, the press box.

But, in 1964 I was playing for an extremely sharp, competent, and innovative coach at the University of Southern California: John McKay. I had been at SC for all of 7 months when we kicked off that 1964 season. We concluded Spring Practice with me as back-up QB to Craig Fertig, a possible wide receiver, and a situational substitute as a defensive back. Fertig had injured his knee during the spring, was in a cast/splint, and status uncertain for the fall. I remained at QB until Fertig received the greenlight, I was switched out to receiver...never to return to QB again.

By November, 1964 we were in contention for the Rose Bowl bid and, in fact, the conference had postponed the voting on the Rose Bowl representative until after our final game with Notre Dame. We played a very physical game against Notre Dame on November 28th and we were the only conference team playing. Notre Dame was undefeated and #1 ranked in the country. If the Trojans could upset the Irish, we could be voted to go to the Rose Bowl.

At halftime the score was Notre Dame 17- USC 0. We moved the ball well in the first half, with no points to show for it. It all changed in the second half. John McKay and his staff were great half-time adjusters. Starting the 4th quarter, Mike Garrett was running well, our defense was shutting down Heisman Trophy winner John Huarte, and receivers Fred Hill, Dave Moton, John Thomas, and Rod Sherman were making catches. With 1:33 left in the game, we were in Irish territory and facing a 4th-and 15 situation. The 15 yards needed had to be for a touchdown.

Coach McKay, put us in a new formation for much of the game. It was a full-house backfield, maximum protection, with two full backs protecting Craig Fertig. On 3rd down; I was on the sideline between Coach McKay & Coach Goux. While Coach McKay was thinking, I blurted out "I think 84 Z Delay will work!". Translation: a young sophomore was calling his own play at the pivotal point of the game. We fail. We won't get the ball back. We fail, we lose the game, We fail; we don't go to the Rose Bowl.

Coach McKay tightened his grip on my arm, leaned towards me and said "go do it!" We sent Garrett in motion to my side of the field, I ran a delayed short post pattern, and go the defender's legs crossed as a cut across the middle, caught the ball and ran untouched into the end zone. There I was hit by the loudest wave of pandemonium that I have ever encountered. It was the closed end of the coliseum and it erupted into what I would describe as a wave of concussions of noise. You couldn't think and, of course, back then there was no spiking of the ball or any type of celebration. I can remember turning towards the Trojan bench—which, in turn, was celebrating and making its way towards me! When I was able to process thoughts again, I can remember gripping the ball and saying to myself: "We're going back to the Rose Bowl"...where it all started-my dream as a kid is now coming true with a catch that I made to help defeat Notre Dame.

The news received 3 hours later while we were at a team dinner ranks right up there with the disillusioning news that a 14 year old boy received from Coach Hunt five years earlier! The conference had voted Oregon State into the Rose Bowl. Football is not about voting. Whether it is the BCS system today or the questionable performance of our conference officials after one of the greatest team performances in USC football history, football is about the scoreboard, not voting.

— ROD SHERMAN

Receiver 1966

My Best Day would be the last game I played at USC against UCLA in 2010. My stats for that game were 212 yards rushing; two touchdowns, and my last play was a 73 yard run.

— ALLEN BRADFORD
Tailback 2010

The score was 13-13 vs Ohio State in 1949 when I inter-cepted a pass. I played center & linebacker; and we scored on that drive for the win.

— **BOYD HACHEN**

Center & Linebacker 1949

My "Best Day" playing for USC was January 1, 1953. We played Wisconsin in the Rose Bowl and won, 7-0!

— **BOB PEVIANI**

Tackle 1953

My Best Day as a Trojan Football player was September 1949. I scored two touchdowns against Navy in the Coliseum; a 30-yard pass play and a 69 yard punt return.

— **JAY ROUNDY**
Offensive Receiver 1949

In 1951 we played Cal with a win of 21-14 with George Bozanic and I making a tackle that ended up on the cover of Life Magazine. Not bad for a Monrovia kid and for George from Lander, Wyoming.

It was always exciting to win and you always felt lousy when you lost. But even with a loss it was exciting knowing that your girlfriend was waiting for you outside the tunnel. Sometimes we would bring the girls an apple from the team basket. To this day, no one is admitting who Debbie Reynolds was waiting for to receive her apple. It had to be one of the guys doing a little Hollywood extra work: Frank Gifford, Harold Hatfield, Al Carmichael or Jim Seals.

That girlfriend and I will be celebrating our 58th wedding anniversary this year.

— **WINSTON GOLLER**
Tackle/End 1951

My husband, Jack Scheliga, who has passed had his proudest days at USC. He was the 1st member of his immediate family to earn a college degree. He went on to earn a master's degree in geology from the university and worked as a water resources expert all over the world.

— **LUAINE SCHELIGA**
wife of Jack Scheliga
1958

I'll never forget the USC VS. Notre Dame game in 1974. USC was favored to win, but Notre Dame was leading 24 to 0 in the second quarter. I was sitting next to a very good friend of mine, Jerry Herbst, who went to USC as well, and we were so down and out that before the second quarter ended we were on our way back to the parking lot where our motor home was parked to drown our sorrows with a little bit of Cutty Sark.

Just before we left the tunnel, we looked back and USC's Anthony Davis had just scored on an 8 yard pass from Haden. So we looked at each other and though maybe that was a turning point for the game. So we went to the motor home, then went back to our seats in the stadium and low and behold USC scored 5 times in the third quarter. One of them was the kickoff return in the fourth quarter with an ending score of 55-24. What a great turn around and what a great game that was! It was indeed something I will never forget.

In fact, Jerry had a close friend from Las Vegas that was a Notre Dame fan and oddly enough he happened to be sitting on the USC side. Well, we could see him from where we were sitting and we could tell that after the second quarter they were quite happy and laughing, but as the third and fourth quarter went on that turned around and they did not stay to see the end of the game.

To top it all off, Jerry Herbst who lives in Las Vegas and belongs to the Las Vegas Country Club, was asked to play golf with Ara Paraseghian, about 2-4 weeks after this game was played. Jerry waiting until Ara Parseghian was on the first tee, about to hit his driver and before he started his swing, Jerry said, "here we go Trojans, here we go!" Ara Parseghian dropped his driver on the ground and looked back at Jerry and said a few words I can't put in writing. We have been through a lot of great USC games and many of them belong on the top of the list, but I do feel that this particular game was at the top.

— **VIC EDELBROCK**
Receiver 1958

I didn't know what was my Best Day until on the plane flight home from the University of Minnesota game I was told by a sportswriter that I had just set a new punt return record. The game had been played in a wind-blown snow storm. Ernie Zambese and I would cross and I'd fake a handoff to him, then go up the right side lines hoping our lineman had a picket ticket line sit up for me to run behind. On both of those attempts I swear both teams and Minnesota's bench met me on the sidelines. I came off the field and sat on the bench and thought about my lack of success and what was the problem.

Every team we played scouted us and knew we ran a picket line, but in the snow storm they couldn't see which way we intended to go, so their lineman just followed our lineman. It was a harsh lesson for me.

Later in the game our defense held them again and Zamp and I were the deep backs again. I called for a return right again, but this time while walking away from the huddle I told Zampese what I thought Minnesota was doing and no matter who caught the ball the other guy was to lead block and we were going left. The ball came to me and Zampese put the only Minnesota player in front of us into about the third row of seats. Marv Goux was the only other player on the left side of the field and I managed to be by him and go on to score.

The run was for 93 yards and a USC record. The previous record was 90 yards that had been set three weeks earlier by our All-American, friend and fraternity brother, Jon Arnett. That was my "Best Day".

As an afterthought about the run, if they had given me credit for the true distance I had run the record would never have been broken again. You see the wind was blowing the snow so hard directly in my face that I didn't know when I crossed the goal line. If it wasn't for the temporary stand in my way I probably would have run through Canada.

— **ERNIE MERK**
Halfback 1955

My Best Days were when I married my wife of 30 years, and when both of my girls were born, but you are requesting a sports performance, so I will go with that.

I had waited for four years to finally get the starting quarterback job at USC in 1977. We were coming off of an 11-1 record in 1976, and a #2 finish in the polls, and had been #1 to begin the 1977 season until we lost to Alabama on National TV, 21-20. Back in those days, we did not have overtime, so we went for the two point conversion and failed. We finished a disappointing 7-4, including the infamous "green jersey" game against Notre Dame in South Bend, 49-19. Joe Montana was a junior that year. Our record was below the early season expectations, but we beat UCLA in our final regular season game to gain a Bluebonnet Bowl Berth in Houston, and knocking the Burins out of the Rose Bowl and any other bowl. Some of the recollection is sketchy, but this is pretty much what I recall.

We fell behind early to UCLA 10-0. I threw two touchdown passes in the second quarter to give us a 20-10 lead at half time. Somehow, we lost momentum and the Bruins stormed back, taking the lead 27-26 in the fourth. We got the ball with about 1:35 to go and on our own 20. We needed a field goal to win it, and we had one time out. We began our final drive with 4 complete passes, and aided by a crucial pass interference play that extended one of the drives. We took our final time out with under 40 seconds to go. I threw a pass with the receiver going out of bounds with 25 seconds to go. We then ran the ball into the middle of the filed, and with time running out, we ran our field goal team out. Frank Jordan kicked the game winning field goal, a 32 yarder, with 2 seconds remaining on the clock. I had dreamed about this all my life growing up a huge Trojan fan. As disappointing as the season was, to end it like that was all worth it. I finished the night 15-25 for 254 yards and 3 touchdowns. I was Chevrolet Player of the Game for ABC TV. We went on to defeat Texas A&M in the Bluebonnet Bowl, where I was voted MVP of the game.

I hope this was what you were looking for. I can always say I was on a USC Team that beat the Bruins. This was my "best day".

— **ROB HERTEL**

Quarterback 1977

As a kid growing up in Texas, football was something that every kid on my block played. I always had a dream of playing for the best college in the United States. My chance came when I had to opportunity to attend a prestige institution like USC. For me to be a part of a host of great running backs like Mike Garrett, O.J. Simpson, Charles White, Marcus Allen and the list goes on which was an honor for me. Also, having the opportunity to be coached by John Robinson one of the best coaches in football and by Charles White (Heisman Trophy Winner) was a dream come true.

If I was to say the most memorable time for me would be my freshman year in 1994 after two weeks of having coach Robinson and Coach White telling me that I was out of shape and they were going to send me back to Texas. Coach Robinson called me into his office two days before the opening day game against the Washington Huskies and told me I was going to have the opportunity to play in the game which featured a running back who was considered to be one of the best backs in the nation at the time named Napoleon Kaufman. For those two days of preparation, I could not sleep. The "Best Day" came when I got my first carry from Quarterback Rob Johnson and I had a run for 16 yards. My heart was racing; I was out of breath from being excited that I was on the same field with Napoleon

Kaufman. On that day, I knew I had become a member of Tailback U Committee of backs at USC. As I look back, on that day I would consider that to be the "Best Day" because I rushed 110 yards. I still have the picture of John Robinson and I hugging one another after the game.

— DELON WASHINGTON
Tailback 1997

There were probably more than just two best days but here are the ones that really stand out for me:

As a walk on quarterback at USC, it was only a dream to ever play for the Trojans. In fact, when I first walked on, QB Coach, Paul Hackett, specifically told me USC recruited the best players in the country and that I would never play. He told me as long as I understood that point I was welcome to be on the team.

One best day was the day (about three years later) that same Paul Hackett took me out to lunch prior to a spring practice session my senior year and told me I would be USC's starting quarterback in the fall (1980). I had beaten out the competition and earned the starting position. What a thrill to go from a complete nobody to the starting quarterback at one of the most prestigious college football schools in the country. I was on cloud nine for a week.

The other best day is an easy one. It occurred about four years later. It's the day my wife of 20 years, Anne. Said yes to marrying me. From that day forward so many other best days occurred...our wedding, the birth of our three children, Vanessa, Claire and Ali and so many great experiences together.

— **GORDON ADAMS**
Quarterback 1980

John McKay was in his very first year as the new head coach at SC in 1960. In 1960, McKay lost his first three games after taking over a Don Clark coached 1959 team that had a 8W and 2L record in 1959. Most of the 1959 players were returning to play in the 1960 season. I was in my sophomore year at USC in 1960 and I was very far down on the team depth chart and only allowed to play a few minutes in two of the first three games that USC lost. We lost to Oregon State, Texas Christian, and Ohio State. McKay's career was in serious jeopardy because of the three loses. McKay decided to shake up his starting team roster. He moved Bill Nelson to the starting quarterback position and he put me in as starting running back against Georgia. Fran Tarkenton was the Georgia starting quarterback. We beat Georgia 10-3. The next week we played California at home and we won that game 27-10. Bill Walsh was Cal's defensive coach. I had a productive game carrying the ball 17 times, gaining 145 yards and breaking loose for a 67 yard touchdown run giving USC the go ahead score in the third quarter. That was my biggest yardage production for USC. The next week we beat Stanford 21-10. USC lost the next two games to Washington and Baylor. The big game of the year was against UCLA who was ranked 11th in the nation and they were supposed to run over USC in 1960. USC beat UCLA 17-6 and years later John McKay ranked this game as the most important game of his career because it saved his job according to John McKay himself, quoted in the LA Times. He gave credit for the win to Bill Nelson, Marlin McKeever, Don Zachik and myself for productive performances. I led the team in rushing and scoring in 1960. My biggest regret was I decided to graduate in 1962. I still had a full year of eligibility and could have played on the USC National Championship team. It was a real honor to have played for USC and I will always be grateful for the opportunity.

— HAL TOBIN

Running Back 1962

As an SC player who never saw any game time; I wanted to respond anyway. I am from Canton, Ohio, and played high school football at Canton McKinley. In the late 50's Canton Coach Wayne Fontes went into coaching and was coaching with John McKay. Wayne recruited me out of Canton McKinley. Between Wayne and my dad's teammate Marv Goux, I got a scholarship to SC.

When I arrived at SC in the fall of 1972, SC had come off a disappointing year (6-4-1). We had easy practices compared to my high school practices and I wondered how we could be successful. But John McKay was a great teacher and our practices were more cerebral than the practices with all the head hanging and screaming from high school.

It amazed me that year when we went 12-0 with all the guys that turned out to be great players from Sam Cunningham to Charles Young, Lynn Swann, Pete Adams, Steve Riley, Anthony Davis, Richard Wood and Charles Phillips.

Now, to answer your question: My best day was January 1, 1973 when we soundly beat Ohio State 42-17. We held Archie Griffin to less than 100 yards and were the first team to be unanimously voted number one at the end of the season.

— **JOHN WEBER**

Defensive Lineman 1975

My Best Day was when I was a junior at USC—we beat Notre Dame on a Saturday in LA and my wife and I got married the next day. The Coaches and players were all there. We have now been married 53 years. She is still the light of my life and is my best friend.

— DICK ENRIGHT

Offensive Lineman 1955

When I joined the USC football team as a walk on in 1997, we had just had a mediocre year after winning the Rose Bowl against Northwestern in 1996. Nevertheless, there was always a sense of pride and swagger at USC. The interesting thing is that I didn't have anything else to compare it against. I was the first in my family to go to college, let alone play sports at the collegiate level.

That being said, I would have to say that my best day at USC Football was my first day at USC Football. Sure it was special to step out of the Coliseum for the first time or start a game or make a big play. However, being a Trojan Football Player means to be something special. The late "Mr. Trojan", Marv Goux, gave a speech after practice that I will paraphrase: "When you wear these jerseys without your name on the back, you begin to appreciate that you don't play for yourself like some of you did when you were in high school. You're playing for those players who played before you: you're playing for the University of Southern California; you are playing for the Alumni and you're playing for the student body."

That speech still gives me goose bumps. FIGHT ON

— PIERRE ZADO

Defensive Lineman 2000

Be your best!

— RONNIE LOTT
Corner/Safety 1980

Every day, Buddy, every day!

— **JUNIOR SEAU**

Linebacker, 1989
Consensus All American and
eight time NFL All Pro

My Best Day was on January 30th, 2012: it was when I signed and put the USC hat on at my national press conference.

— ZACK BANNER

Offensive Tackle 2015

The first time walking through the tunnel at the Coliseum in a Trojan uniform.

— MICHAEL HELFRICH
Safety 2013

Being able to play for USC Football, and now for USC volleyball has been my best day so far.

— JB GREEN

Wide Receiver 2014

I have many strong memories about playing football at USC. Many may write about a particular game, a particular play or a specific meeting. However, in retrospect, I think my best day came from turning a low point into a turning point. It is fair to say that I had my fair share of injuries. In particular, my left knee had a tendency to dislocate no matter how much tape the trainers applied and no matter how many how many different types of braces the ortho-pedist modified. I had surgery between my sophomore and junior season

To try to fix the problem. After rehabbing my knee be-tween fall and spring practice, my knee dislocated again, this time while I was just running straight ahead. Nobody fell into it, it didn't get stuck in the turf and I didn't twist it in any way. In short, my knee just had a structural de-fect that made is susceptible to dislocate. I recall leaving practice, on crutches, rather devastated as the rehab pro-cess had already been long. I thought things had hit rock bottom at that point. I recall going to see an on-campus screening of Platoon. That brought on a new level of de-pression. After leaving the show, I crutched over to where my moped was parked, only to find that someone had stolen it. That was about the lowest point in my college career. At that point, I figured the only thing I could control was my performance in the classroom. I crutched over to the library and spent several hours studying for an economics exam. It was probably the best study session I've ever had. For some reason, I was able to focus on studying since it was an escape from the other aspects of my life at the time. Throughout law school and my professional career, I've often faced difficult issues and stressful situations. I've always been able to attack them with the same clarity of that night. One thought runs through my head as times get difficult or stressful—no matter how challenging the situation, it isn't more difficult than the struggles I went through during football and especially that night.

— CHUCK EBERTIN

Center 1988

My Best Day was our opener at Boston College on Labor Day 1988. It was a close game during the 3rd quarter and we were attempting a field goal. Along with being the punter, I doubled as the holder on field goals. The snap came back high and over my head. I jumped up and caught the ball in mid-air and started to roll out. As I neared the sideline I threw the ball toward one of my wingbacks (Aaron Emanuel). Aaron out jumped about five defenders and came down in the corner for a touchdown. The crowd of about 70,000 became eerily quiet and the feeling I got was so surreal like everything was moving in slow-motion. I will remember that day for the rest of my life.

— **CHRIS SPERLE**
Punter/holder 1988

Like all other athletes, I faced some adverse situations throughout my athletic career. After being an offensive player throughout high-school, as well as in the beginning of my college career, I finally found a home on the defensive side of the ball as a defensive lineman. This was a position which I was not familiar with, but I was eager to learn it and get on the field.

Playing on the defensive line provided a whole new football experience for me. The transition required plenty of hard work, but it was exciting and I enjoyed watching myself progress as a football player. After hours upon hours of grueling hard work, my best day arrived. It was time for me to make my college debut. I was standing there on the sidelines, and then I heard my coach yell my name. He grabbed my jersey, told me to get in, and I sprinted onto the field. The feeling I had was indescribable. My dream was to play football for the Trojans, and when that day finally arrived, it was my best day.

FIGHT ON!

— **ZACK KUSNIR**
Defensive Lineman 2012

I was very fortunate to be a member of a really good team. We all had the same objective: to play as a team; help each other; and feel good about the outcome. We really wanted to win, as every competitor does.

I was an important member of this good team. Being the offensive center and able to snap the ball a distance of 17 yards to Des Koch, who led the nation in punt distances, and being the middle linebacker in a very stout defense, we ranked high in national statistics.

As for my best day, I'd have to say it was against Stanford University (1952) and Bob Mathias. He was such an awesome athlete. I was assigned to a "man to man" defensive status in that wherever Bob went, I went with him. I did that and we were able to limit Stanford's offense. This led to me being selected as the "Defensive Player of the Game" for the Trojans.

— **DICK PETTY**

Center/Linebacker 1952

I grew up in a family that have been Trojan fans for as long as I can remember. 1939-43 we lived in Fresno and every year USC participated in the West Coast Relays and they usually won.

I was eight year old when I went to the New Year's Parade in Pasadena in 1939 and then the Rose Bowl Game between USC and Duke where USC won 7-3. My brother Bob played for USC in 1946-1949.

One of my best days was when I received a letter from Jeff Cravath–head football coach at USC, offering me a full ride scholarship to attend and play football. What a thrill, a once in a lifetime dream come true-becoming a TROJAN. Another best day would be playing in the Rose Bowl game in 1953 and beating Wisconsin 7-0. I did have a small contribution by catching 3 passes from our quarterback Rudy Buckich – MVP.

— **DON STILLWELL**

Receiver 1952

I will have to say that my Best Day came when we were trailing UCLA in the final two minutes of the game, 12-7. With both teams in 1969 being undefeated in the final game of the season, the winner would be going to the Rose Bowl. There was 1:32 left in the game, I caught a 32 yard touchdown pass to put us up 14-12. We went on to beat Michigan 10-3 in the 1970 Rose Bowl.

— SAM DICKERSON

Wide Receiver 1969

(as told by Hanks wife) his Best Day was the day he received a football scholarship from USC. He was so thrilled and proud to be a Trojan. There were many memorable tackles and plays and wins.

— JAYNE SLADE
for Hank Slade 1958

I was fortunate enough, during my time at USC, to accomplish many personal goals; to play in the (then) pac-8, to play in a sold-out Coliseum, to play at Notre Dame Stadium in South Bend, to be a member of a National Championship Team, to play in the Rose Bowl and to compete against some of the best football programs in the country (Alabama, Nebraska, Oklahoma, Arkansas and Notre Dame).

If I were required to identify one personal "Best Day" experience, it would be our game against Notre Dame in 1972, my senior year. Not only was the USC vs Notre Dame series the greatest intersectional rivalry in college football, it was the final game of the season and, for the seniors, the last game we would ever play in the Coliseum. A lot was riding on the outcome. We were undefeated and ranked number 1 in all the polls. We had already clinched a Rose Bowl Bid by virtue of winning the Pacific 8 conference, but, as a team we were much more focused on the possibility of winning the National Championship. Notre Dame was also highly ranked and we had pulled off an incredible upset the year before in South Bend. I'm quite certain they had revenge on their minds. They would've loved nothing more than to spoil our National Championship bid.

The kickoff was scheduled for 1:00pm and the Coliseum was standing room only. The game was on national television and the stadium was buzzing with all the typical trappings of a giant media event; cameras, audio and video technicians everywhere, celebrities lining the field, sideline reporters and, of course, the Goodyear blimp. Team wise, due to a rash of late season injuries, we were depleted in numbers along the defense line. Several defensive linemen were in street clothes and those of us who started the game knew we were in for a long afternoon against a very physical opponent whose forte was to run the ball right through you.

We won the coin toss and elected to receive the ball. We returned the opening kickoff for a touchdown and immediately had a little bit of "breathing room". The first half was every bit as physical as we expected from a Notre Dame team but we played solid football and took a lead into the locker room at halftime. Half time was uneventful and Coach McKay was never a big "rah-rah" guy in the locker room. Following the intermission the "slugfest" continued and we, as a team, were slightly less productive on offense than we normally were. As a team, we had never been behind in the second half of a game all year, and our closest victory margin was 9 points. We were only up by 2, and I remember all these years later with clarity how we all looked at each other and without anyone saying a word we communicated a sense of confident resolution that we

would get the job done regardless of what was required.
On the next kickoff our special teams unit returned the ball over 100 yards for a touchdown. We were now ahead by 9 points and they had worked so hard to get within striking distance, and then it was gone in one play.

The score ended up being more one-sided than it felt playing it, the final score was 45-23. We went on to the 1973 Rose Bowl where we defeated Woody Hayes and the Ohio State Buckeyes by the score of 42-17. We were crowned National Champions and became the first team to be voted unamously number one by both the AP and UPI voters. We as a team, received many more trophies and awards but, to the players, none were more important than the rings we received from the NCAA for winning the National Championship.

A great many of the lessons that, to me, are the embodiment of football were experienced by us that day. The value of perseverance; never giving up and competing as hard as you can for as long as you can. The value of teamwork; without the contributions of all three units of our team we would not have been able to prevail. And, finally, the value of believing in yourselves and having the confidence to do whatever is necessary to achieve your goal.
I have always been proud to be a Trojan. I was proud and privileged to be a part of the 1972 team that both ESPN

and the highly esteemed sportscaster Keith Jackson voted the best college football team of all time. I was particularly proud to be a member of that team's defense which allowed only 14 touchdowns during the regular season, only 94 yards per game rushing and only 136 yards per game through the air. Never did that defense shine more brightly than it did on December 2, 1972 in the Los Angeles Memorial Coliseum against the University of Notre Dame. That was my best day as a USC Trojan.

— **GEORGE FOLLETT**

Defensive Line 1972

It was a long, tiresome bus trip from the airport in Austin, Texas. We had a delayed flight and were tired from a long week of practice. I sat next to our head coach, Jess Hill, in the 1st two seats of the chartered bus. Coach Hill was talking about different game plans and strategies, and as the quarterback, I was used to these impromptu conversations. I was one of the first players in the hotel with our team manager waiting for our assignments. As tired as we all were, the next words out of concierge mouth are something that will be with me my whole life. In a sheepish demeanor, he said, "I have arranged for all your team members except for your three Negro Players (The term African America had not been established yet)We have arranged lodging for them at another location." I looked at Coach Hill in disbelief and shock, and he was as stunned as we were. Mild mannered Coach Hill was very angry. After a long, glaring pause, he said, "We, the team, will not be staying at this hotel, we are a team, not divided in any manner whatsoever, and that not only would we not stay at this hotel, we won't use the chain of hotels that bear the same name and defamatory policies. He then ushered all of the Trojan football team back into the buses.

Team members were puzzled as to what occurred, however once the ugly incident was revealed to them,

World War II would have paled in comparison. Our mood ran from disbelief to outrage. The anger festered throughout the next day's practice and we couldn't wait for game day.

The Saturday game was our first night game, and we were 14 point underdogs. The Texas fans were wild. We won the coin toss, and without going into play-by-play analysis, most emphatically, that history was made that night. C.R. Roberts, one of our African American players, was a fullback and he broke the Southern Conference rushing record by rambling for 263 yard, scoring 3 touchdowns, a record that would last for 2 ½ decades before another USC back, Ricky Bell, would eclipse C.R.s amazing fete. Time and again, Lou Byrd and Hillard Hill, our two other African American teammates, would make key blocks, to aid CR in his record breaking performance. The final score: USC 44- Texas 20.

During my USC career I was lucky enough to play in a Rose Bowl, represent USC in the East-West game, but those were secondary to that historic night in Austin, Texas.

After showering, we were greeted by Texas fans wanting CR's autograph. A bittersweet ending to which I say is my most memorable night in my athletic career.

Darryl Royal, the University of Texas head coach, would after the next few years, start recruiting African

American Athletes. Enough cannot be said for C.R. Roberts, now an accountant, Lou Byrd, a Councilman, and Hillard Hill, a private business owner, for their historic efforts in the beginning stages of abolition of racial discrimination, coming 11 months after Rosa Parks said "no."

— **FRANK HALL**
Quarterback 1954

My Best Day of football at USC was the 1965 game versus the University of Washington. Washington had beaten us in the past couple of years and they were a tough opponent. Coach McKay was on all of us, and on me after an article on my dad (who coached with McKay) said he taught me everything I knew.

I was nervous, because Washington was a tough team and really like to "spear" people with their helmets as they were tackling. Washington banged our dressing room door, and screaming things at us as they passed the hall.

I remember the first play of the game, as if it was yesterday. I got into the huddle and called, "open b right, 64-y out on go" A voice in the huddle (Ron Yary) said "on hike". I then said, "on hike, on hike", as it should have been called, and we got to the line and ran the pass play and it was complete. The game was on. I can remember recovering a fumble (Mike Garrett) and fumbling once on the snap from center. After my miscue, we held Washington very well, and I thought that it was a turning point in the game.

At the end of the first half, Coach McKay changed the play and there was not enough time to let everyone know, so I called out "red". I pivot to fake the pass to Mike Garrett; but half the team went with the old play and it was mass confusion. I kept the ball trying to pass to someone.

As I ran a while and nearing the goal line, there we two defenders coming for me. I tucked the ball and prepared to get hit really hard. I prepared for the ensuing collision, with both defenders, who were famous for hitting you in the face mask. Much to my surprise I flipped over them into the end zone for the touchdown. And with the extra point, it was 14-0 at half.

We played well in the 2nd half, with great plays from Mike Hull & Rod Sherman. We won 34-0, a monster win at that time.

I was 11 for 11, which set an NCAA record that stood for 30 years. I remember Coach McKay left his hat on the bus, which I wore for several weeks (but not to practice) to remind me of the best game that was so very memorable.

Fight On

— **TROY WINSLOW**

Quarterback 1965

My Best Day was the USC vs Washington game. The ball came straight at me and I picked it up to change the game for our win.

— ANTHONY BROWN

Corner 2014

I am fortunate to have three Best Days while playing for the USC Trojans. Playing at USC was an incredible experience that is hard to describe. In many ways the big stage, the competition and the success of the football program makes one feel you're part of something very special that few get to actually go through. On the other hand, one realized that football is first AND everything else is a distant second.

My sophomore year my dream goal became a reality when we played Ohio State in the 1985 Rose Bowl. The Buckeyes were driving and gave the ball to Keith Byers, where I got under him for the "hit of the game"...I am thankful to the boys upfront who let me flow to the play without getting blocked...

My junior year we played the Bruins at the Coliseum. We had lost to them the last 2 years, and they were driving down the field to go up 20-10. I blitzed against the coaches decision, and leaped over the lead block; hitting my helmet on the ball by the tailback who is trying to jump the goal line. The RB coughed up the ball, Marcus Cotton caught the ball and ran it out to the 50 yard line. Our QB, Rodney Peete drove us to a score and we won beating UCLA in the Coliseum...it could be the greatest play in my entire life...

My senior year Illinois came out to the Coliseum to play us in the 1st game of the season. This is my senior year, and I wanted an opportunity to play in the NFL. I realized every game is important. After the game I was not aware of how many tackles I had for that day against the Illini. Tim Tessalone, our sports information director relayed to me that I made 23 tackles, and that it was a USC record. I am proud to say that record still stands to this very day... Hopefully, someone will break it soon...

— SAM ANNO

Linebacker 1986

(As told by wife, Ester Cramer) Stan's best day remembered was when he was invited to come to USC in 1946 after serving three years in the Army, much of that time on the front lines in Germany. He had been named "player of the year" while playing football for his outfit in Europe. When he arrived at USC he found that there were 80 ends who were trying to make the position. The end coach was Bill Fisk, and out of the many trying out, Stan was chosen as left end on a freshman football team that competed with many of the Junior Colleges. USC Freshmen were indeed outstanding. Stan went on to become the first head coach as Cerritos College, then Head Coach at Mt. San Antonio College. All of this was possible due to playing at USC.

— **STAN CRAMER**

by his wife Ester
Defensive End 1946

There were many Best Days at USC but two stand out amongst many because it meant the 1962 National Championship.

At Iowa, I scored the only touchdown in a 7-0 USC victory.

In 1962, January 1st- Rose Bowl again number 2 ranked and undefeated Wisconsin. (USC was ranked number 1) I scored a touchdown around right end with my junior college friend, Jay Clark, throwing a key block as I turned to corner.

— RON HELLER

Running Back 1962

I've been blessed to have played in over 200 NFL games that included two Pro Bowls, two Super Bowls as well as at the collegiate level, I played in two Rose Bowls. I have the injuries to prove it…

My Best Day as a Trojan: I recall after beating Notre Dame in South Bend, Coach Marv Goux, "Mr. Trojan" had all the seniors come back out of the locker room to focus on the score board. He said, "You are a special group" because this was the first time USC had beaten them four years straight! (1981) Fight On!

— **ROY FOSTER**

Offensive Guard 1981

What makes a Trojan different? A Trojan is built from the inside out, a Trojan is a winner. A Trojan may fall once or twice, but a Trojan will get up every time and never ever give up, even when down by three touchdowns, or even when facing a more craftier opponent like infection. We have a strong core belief that defines who we are, which can be applied to any situation, any endeavor, any occupation, and also in our relationships with others. We will be successful with the occupation that we choose. The same skills, energy, faithfulness, diligences that were applied once as a young adult at a great university of USC, will be applied in life. My best day; continuing to be a strong and loving husband to my wife Olivia, I want to continue to be the man she can love and respect always, my best day would include my relationship with my son Garrett, being involved in his life every day, helping him to grow into a strong and honorable man that someday will be blessed like I have been and will understand what it means to be a Trojan.

— MIKE ROTH

Center 1982

I had the opportunity to play football at USC for a short time back in 1945, I was in the Navy NROTC program and was transferred from the University of Redlands football to USC in the middle of the 1945 football season. My Best Day was on January 1, 1946, when we played the University of Alabama in the Rose Bowl. We lost, but the coach put in the third string to play during the last 2 or 3 minutes of the game. We blocked an Alabama punt, and I picked up the ball and ran it into the end zone for a touchdown. WHAT A THRILL!! I'll remember it for my whole life as "My Best Day".

A few weeks later a friend of mine mailed me an article that said I had made the first and last touchdowns in the 1945 college football season; both in the Rose Bowl. It was ironic.

— CHUCK CLARK

Defensive End 1945

I have been blessed is so many ways and have so many memories and Best Days playing football at USC. It is hard to name just one Best Day.

Starting at guard in the 1963 Rose Bowl game against Wisconsin as a sophomore was great. I had just turned 19 two days before the game. This game would be at the top of my list. We won the game and the National Championship. I celebrated my birthday and our victory with my family and friends after the game.

Another Best Day would be receiving a call after the 1964 season and hearing that I had just been selected on the AP first team All American Team.

— BILL FISK

Guard 1964

My USC Best Day was during a spring practice game because I never got into a real game. In 1954 guys played both ways, and you could go all game with only 15 or 20 guys. I was USC's "Rudy", and I got a brief write up in the L.A. Times Sports Section for what was my Best Day as a player. I caught 3 passes, which was a fair total in those days. The nice words were probably for what was not really a catch, but the ball "stuck" in the crook of my arm when I had 3 or 4 guys hanging on me. It just looked like a catch. In that same game I didn't see C.R. Roberts just standing there as a middle linebacker and I ran into him full blast. He must have thought he was attacked by a mosquito, he didn't even flinch! I consoled my lack of game time playing with the fact that as a scrub I got to play 3 times as much as everyone else, we played the 1st, 2nd and 3rd string. I do wish I had gotten to play one or two plays on a Fall Saturday like Rudy did, but I loved football and had the time of my life.

— **JIM WILKERSON**
Wide Receiver 1954

Bobby Robertson Best Day was a defensive play against UCLA during a scoreless tie in 1939. He broke up a fourth-down pass from the one-yard line that halted a Bruin drive, preserving USC's unbeaten record and sent the Trojans into the 1940 Rose Bowl against Tennessee. USC beat Tennessee 14-0 for USC's fourth National Championship. Bobby was nicknamed the "$100,000 kid" and he loved football his whole life, and was an avid USC fan.

— **BOBBY ROBERTSON**

as told by his widow
Halfback 1940

I played USC football in the early 1960's and my life has been interesting, rewarding and just life. I was blessed to play on the 1962 National Championship team. I survived a nine hour battle in Vietnam on September 4th, 1967 against 4000 N Vietnamese Regulars while serving with the US Marine Corp, was a White House Staff Assistant, coached the freshman football team while in graduate school and was a partner 21 years with two of the largest Executive Recruiting Firms in the world. I have also experienced the down side of life; I lost a wonderful son in Iraq on November 11, 2004 and my wife of 32 years died of cancer in January 2008. However, the best day(s) of my life was/were being witness to the births of my three children. Being a participant to the miracle of life is certainly my "Best Day."

— **EDWARD BLECKSMITH**

Defensive Back 1964

So many wonderful and great memories from my time spent at USC. When I get together with my former teammates we always talk about the camaraderie we had. The greatest memories all took place on Howard Jones Field. We didn't know it at the time but every day in practice we were competing against "future greats"!

The competitions we had on the field...only to end the day as "Trojan Brothers". When I arrived at USC I was playing with the likes of Tony Boselli and my last year was with Carson and company. So, to answer your question, my fondest and most precious memories of my time spent at USC was on Howard Jones Field. I had the privilege of playing with some of the best players in the nation and I played for some of the greatest coaches ever.

My brother in law, Kevin Arbet, was on two national championship teams after I had already graduated and he and I both feel the same way about our fondest memories of being at USC.

As I am writing this, I just remembered a great day of football and Coach Robinson stopped practice to give us a 7 minute break...in came trash cans full of popcycles. This was an awesome treat on a hot, hard day at work on Howard Jones Field. Fight On

— **DOUG ROME**
Offensive Tackle 1996

I have had too many Best Days to remember, but a few that stand out would be: the days I became a believer in Jesus Christ; the day I married my wife, the birth of our four daughters and the birth of our first granddaughter (hopefully many more grandchildren)

— DON MOSEBAR

Center 1982
Consensus All-American

There were many, obviously coving all the possible emotional ranges, but at the end of the day, all I can remember was that it was an awesome time in my life. I could say it was when I met my wife, or signed my letter of intent, or freshman year that I started, BUT; there is one day, which will always stick out in my mind. Sad thing is, it was a day in which USC TIED San Diego State.

Four weeks prior to the 1991 Fall season I was diagnosed with Testicular Cancer. I had several surgeries, and had a brief, successful four-week round of Chemotherapy. I returned to classes, but sat out the season. After spring workout, I was pronounced fit to return to full football duties. Still not my best day....

I spent that summer working out hard, attending summer school and working. I worked out closely with Michael Mooney and Rory Brown, and we all pushed each other very hard.

In the fall, I was in great shape but did not expect to start. I was backup center, and worked hard on special teams. I knew I liked to hit and could take a blow, so I gave the wedge-kickoff return a try and this is where my best day came.

USC's 1st game was in San Diego, and my mom traveled from Houston to watch my game. I don't remember much about the game, other than Marshall Faulk running wild and around the corner at least twice on long touch-down runs, but the one thing that will always stick out, which constitutes what made up the best day was a play that to many if not all others would be forgotten.

USC scored !! That meant an extra point, and even as I type, tears and tingles hit me! I was ready; I lined up as the right end, and standing somewhat at a horizontal angle behind me was none other than my summer workout buddy, Mike Mooney. We locked hands, then the ball was snapped and the kick was good. I don't even think that anyone even rushed from that side, I hugged Mike and we ran off the field. Coach Larry Smith gave me a high five as I ran off the field, I am sure I had tears of joy in mine, and I know my mom did as well. I was back! In putting it all together, we did that same thing on the field 4 more times. Even with a tie at the end of the game, nothing could sway me from remembering it as the best day while at USC.

— **DAVID APOLSKIS**

Special Teams 1991

My Best Days:

• The day I accepted Jesus Christ as my Savior on 7/29/1979.

• The day I married my wife 57 years ago.

• At USC: in 1953 Rose Bowl Game. USC vs Wisconsin: I recovered the fumble that set up the Rudy Buckich to Al Carmichael for the only score. We beat Wisconsin 7-0 and were National Champions.

— **BOB HOOKS**

End 1953

The accomplishments I made on the field and being recognized as a good player from the USC Coaches was my Best Day. It was fun to compete with the top athletes and being there right with them competitively; at least until my injuries took over. The USC training staff was very good and took great care of me.

— BRANDON KULA
Fullback 2010

I held out as long as I could, I was a certified, confirmed bachelor. Life had been kind but incomplete. I had known a lot of beautiful women in my lifetime. I had been engaged a twice as I recall. In 1999 I crossed paths with someone I had met 30 years prior. I did not know at the time she had been divorced for eight years. She did not tell me. Well, she did not know I was interested. One year after seeing her, her brother, Clifford Branch (my former teammate-Oakland Raiders) came to my house and I asked about his sister. Elaine was her name, and Cliff broke the news that she was a divorcee and had been for years. I immediately asked him for her phone number. I asked her to be my date in Las Vegas to a birthday party. I tried to get her to elope with me in Vegas, and even offered to give her my Super Bowl ring as a wedding present. She turned me down and we dated for 2 years. On June 30, 2001 we were married; I was 52 years old and never married. I am a stroke patient. Since getting married I am no longer on high blood pressure medicine. Elaine is a keeper. To make my best days the absolute best we enjoy visiting our children for her 1st marriage, Sohn and Shane and my kids from a previous relationship, Tyler and Danielle. God is good.

— CLARENCE DAVIS,
Running Back 1979

I think if I have to chose one best day it would be the day that I married my wife. It's been over 35 years-and obviously it is not easy-we have been through some tough times; however, our relationship has enabled us to work everything out to our satisfaction. We have four wonderful children- all extremely conscientious, hard working, confident, honest, and bright. Because of them, we feel truly blessed.

– NORM CHOW,
USC Assistant Football Coach 2001-2004

What at question! Life is important and this question definitely raises the bar on the "why it really is". As you know, this question has taken me considerable time to answer as I have had so many great days that I could speak of…the very day the gift of life was granted to me…the very day I realized that I was loved by my father and mother…the very day I experienced the realization of true love with an incredible young lady…and the very day she became my wife…as well as every special day that God would bless her and I with three amazing children that I knew deep in my soul a love that words could not express…so many great friends and moments that I could also speak of…However, if I am to honestly address the question at hand I can unequivocally say that one day stands out amongst all the others as it was the day that defined the "how and why I live".

It was, not too long ago, February 29th, 2004…the very day I heard my Heavenly Father shout into my soul…"Behold, I have shown you the ways of life, my joy and countenance is now upon you!"

– VICTOR RAKHSHANI,
Wide Receiver 1980

As a former walk-on for the USC Trojans in the spring of 1989, I did not feel that my story for this book would be relevant or significant. A couple of weeks ago I played in the first annual Lane Kiffin Golf Tournament and Coto De Caza Country Club. After a great day of gold with friends, I ran into a lot of guys that I had played football with at USC and we started discussing this book. I want to thank Shane Foley, Mike Salmon, Mazio Royster and Sunny Bird for helping me realize I had something to contribute, so here goes…

In the spring of 1989 as a sophomore, I was without a major and a member of the Delta Tau Delta Fraternity. After a huge party I ran into a friend from high school, who said he was sick of the party scene and wanted to do something more constructive with his time. He said he wanted to walk on to the football team, and I immediately told him I was in!

I moved out of the Frat house, went to the gym and began running for 3 months. This preparation time was "top secret" as we did not want any of our friends or family to know what we were doing. The next step was convincing Ray Dorr and Bobby April to allow us the opportunity to try out during the spring. This was the most difficult task of the entire experience, but staying after them and bugging them daily paid dividends after about a month. The stage was set…

That spring was out of this world. After the first couple days of conditioning were behind us, things moved quickly.

I was walking on as a receiver and enjoying daily drills against players such as Mark Carrier and Junior Seau who made sure I knew what it felt like to play against a Division I powerhouse every day.

After the spring was over I was instructed to come back and meet with Coach Dorr at the end of summer. At the meeting I was informed that I was to remain on the team; obviously an incredible day for me that I will never forget. That season was my "Best Day" as a USC Football Player. Just some small highlights of that season:

Scott Ross tackling me so hard that I thought he left his facemask in my back for three days.

Junior Seau coming ten yards off on a blitz and Reggie Perry snapping the ball before I cleared the line while in motion and Junior absolutely KILLING me. And as I was waking up from being knocked out momentarily, our leader Larry Smith looking over me and simply stating, "I see you met Junior".

The perfectly thrown ball from Reggie on a deep post corner right over the outstretched hands of Mark Carrier in the corner of the end zone for a scout team touchdown.
Running out of the tunnel of the Coliseum and hearing the crowd is a memory that will last forever.

Beating Michigan in the Rose Bowl (Bo Schembechler's final game) and getting a Rose Bowl Ring.

AWESOME!

The valuable lessions that I leared during this time of my life have influenced me greatly as a father, husband and business owner. They were great days indeed. FIGHT ON!

– MATT HURRAY,
Wide Receiver

It was in 1942 when we beat California by two touchdowns and one was a 70 yard plus run by Mickey McArdle leading interference.

I blocked the last man that could have tackled him and we went the rest of the way to pay dirt.

– BILL SEIXAS,
Guard

1)   September 20, 1986 USC vs Baylor

The Trojans traveled into Waco, Texas that weekend for a big game! It was a great match up in a loud Baylor stadium. Statistically, we were beat up pretty bad that game, but never once gave up. Down 7-0 with 15 seconds remaining in the first half, Tim McDonald ran back a fumble 99 yards for a touchdown and we tied the game at 7. Our defense kept us in the game the second half and enabled our offense to have decent field position going into the last drive of the game. As we drove deeper into Baylor's end of the field, the rain began to fall and continued to fall harder. With 2 seconds left in the game, we called a time out and set up for a 32 yard field goal. As expected, Baylor made use of their last time out to "ice" the kicker, me, and enable the rain to have some time to fall harder. The rain began to come down so hard that it took two of the TV cameras out that were televising the game and the rain looked like static on the TV screen. Our field goal team stayed focused and Scott Brennan and Kevin McLean executed the snap and hold perfectly, enabled me to make a 32 yard field goal to win the game 17-14.

2)   November 29, 1986- USC vs Notre Dame

Although a sad day for Trojan Football and especially the seniors on the football team, I was blessed with the opportunity to kick a 60 yard field goal on the last play of the first half. To this day it is still a USC record and tied for the Pac 10 (now Pac-12) record. I also kicked a 48 and 21 yard field goal that day. We lost the game 38-37 and were booed off the field by our student body.

– DON SHAFER,
Placekicker 1986

My best day was and is...EVERY DAY I awaken with the same old stars in my eyes and hope still springs eternal---28,752 days so far (as of April 19, 2004), counting 19 leap years.

– JOHN HALL,
Sports Writer

My Best Day is every day, because it's the gift of life that God has given us.

– BRIAN KELLY,
Corner

My first day at the University was February 1st, 1960. John McKay gave me a great opportunity. I coached with some great men and friends, and coached hundreds of great young men for twenty years. I associated with countless alums and many faculty members. It was a good life. My two sons graduated from USC. I worked for Nick Pappas-what a great human being! To find one day and make it a best day is impossible. It's even hard to pick out a best year. Like the mother with man y children- I have favorites, but I love them all the same. I live near the University so I get to see many players at carious events. It is still exciting to remember them as students and to follow their exciting lives. Their Best Day was my Best Day. It has been great to be a Trojan. FIGHT ON!

– DAVE LEVY,
USC Assistant Coach 1960-1975

I have had a lot of "Best Days" in my life. However, the day John McKay offered me a football scholarship at USC profoundly influenced the rest of my life.

The quality of a USC education and football program provided me with the expertise and passion to pursue a career in couching.

I coached football in high school, college and the NFL for a total of 42 years. We won two national championships at USC, two super bowls with the Dallas Cowboys. More important that the victories, however, were the relationships I formed with the coaches and players throughout the years.

I owe so much to USC and John McKay for that special day he offered me a scholarship that influenced the rest of my life.

– HUDSON HOUCK,
Center, USC 1962-1065
Coach 1970-1971 & 1976-1989

After my father left Long Beach Poly to coach at USC, I became a diehard fan even though I was only five or six years old. I grew up, received an athletic scholarship and spent four years on the team and graduated. I considered myself a stronger fan than a player until 1974, when we played #1 Notre Dame.

A day I won't forget was about to happen. I was suited up, it was half time and we were down 24-6. Most of the team fit in the locker room, but a few of us stood in the hallway, myself included. Coach McKay spoke loud and enthusiastically to us about how he wanted us to get out there and fight our way back into this game. He meant every word and it was encouraging and heartfelt. We took the field, fought and clawed our way to take a 42-24 lead with six minutes left in the game. Then the moment I'll never forget came when the coach said to me " you are going in Johnny". I was thrilled to be part of a historic football game. This was beyond belief!! We won 55-24 and this was my biggest USC moment.

– JOHN LEVY,
1974